HOW TO BE
A
CONSCIOUS
EATER

Making Food Choices That Are Good for You, Others, and the Planet

SOPHIE EGAN

Illustrated by Iris Gottlieb

WORKMAN PUBLISHING · NEW YORK

TO MY BOYS, AIDEN AND ELLIOT.

Your belly kicks kept me company all those early hours in my writing cave, and now your smiles light up my world every day.

Library of Congress Cataloging-in-Publication Data is available.

ISBN 978-1-5235-0738-2

Design by Rae Ann Spitzenberger

Workman books are available at special discounts when purchased in bulk for premiums and sales promotions as well as for fund-raising or educational use. Special editions or book excerpts can also be created to specification. For details, contact the Special Sales Director at the address below or send an email to specialmarkets@workman.com.

Workman Publishing Co., Inc.
225 Varick Street
New York, NY 10014-4381
workman.com

WORKMAN is a registered trademark of Workman Publishing Co., Inc.

Printed in China
First printing February 2020

10 9 8 7 6 5 4 3 2 1

Disclaimer: The author is not a doctor or medical professional. Before making any changes to your diet, consult a professional health care practitioner. Neither the author nor the publisher shall be liable or responsible for any loss, injury, or damage allegedly arising from any information or suggestions contained in this book. This book is the product of Sophie Egan as an individual, not a spokesperson for The Culinary Institute of America.

CONTENTS

INTRODUCTION iv

═══ PART 1 ═══

STUFF THAT COMES FROM THE GROUND
1

═══ PART 2 ═══

STUFF THAT COMES FROM ANIMALS
81

═══ PART 3 ═══

STUFF THAT COMES FROM FACTORIES
159

═══ PART 4 ═══

STUFF THAT'S MADE IN RESTAURANT KITCHENS
223

10 SOURCES I TRUST 258

GLOSSARY 259

ACKNOWLEDGMENTS 262

INDEX 264

ABOUT THE AUTHOR 270

INTRODUCTION

I f you feel like there are more questions than answers about food right now, you're not alone. It's bananas out there at the grocery store. (Bananas: still healthy, BTW.) One day it seems like eggs are bad, then the next day they're good. One day we give up coffee because of cancer scares, the next a report comes out telling us it's the key to a long life. The whole (mis)information melee is enough to make you throw your hands in the air, eat Hot Pockets, and hope for the best.

And that's all before you toss in personal politics. Should you forgo almonds over concerns about water use? If you do, you'll be passing up a healthy snack. Or how about fish? Eating them can sometimes mean depleting available species and harming the oceans, but skipping them means missing out on well-documented health benefits, including brain development for babies.

Often food information is presented in silos: Getting caught up in which grass-fed beef label is best for the life of the cow, for example, misses the point that too much beef—of any variety—isn't so hot for us or the planet. (Actually, cows are making the planet much hotter. More on that later.) These things can't be viewed in a vacuum.

Chances are, though, if you care about what goes into your body, you have at least started to care about how what you eat affects the individuals who grew it and the land where it was grown. For example, if you're paying attention to organic labels on your produce out of concerns for your health, you may have also learned about pesticides harming farmworkers and the surrounding habitat.

This book aims to clear up the confusion in the form of a one-stop reference, broken down into all the major sources of food: (1) stuff that comes from the ground, (2) stuff that comes from animals, (3) stuff that comes from factories, and (4) stuff that's made in restaurant kitchens. It's organized in descending order, from a health standpoint, of foods to eat the most of (whole, plant-based foods, which come from the ground) to stuff to eat the least of (generally speaking, foods you eat when dining away from home tend to be less healthy than those you cook yourself). All together, you'll gain bottom-line answers to the most top-of-mind questions about conscious eating. Nutrition and environmental science and social movements evolve over time, but by and large, the guidance in this book is evergreen—it's meant to help you over the long haul. Embracing it should bring you peace of mind for the foreseeable future that you are nourishing yourself and your family in the best ways possible—and leaving as positive a footprint as you can on the people and places behind your food.

Beyond the sixty topics I tackle individually, this book should help you in the big picture by offering a memorable, thorough framework for solving a problem that so many of us are facing: how to simplify the complexity of making daily food choices we can feel good about. That is, the *Conscious Eater Checklist*: good for you, good for others, good for the planet.

IS IT GOOD FOR YOU? This means good for the *whole* you. Food that is nutritious, safe, wholesome—food that does a body good. This lens recognizes that food plays an emotional role in our lives, and a social role in our families and our communities. Information is merely one of many pieces that make up the complex puzzle of our decision to eat something or not, and how much; also critical are the cultural elements of each decision, such as tradition, nostalgia, familiarity, and the delight of discovering new flavors. So, "good for you" largely concerns your health, but it also relates to your happiness.

IS IT GOOD FOR OTHERS? This is about leaving the best possible mark on the animals and people affected across our food systems, from the growing/raising/producing to the harvesting/processing/transporting and the preparing/serving/disposing of each item you consume.

IS IT GOOD FOR THE PLANET? This involves making choices that do not damage, and when possible even restore, the ecosystems impacted by food production. Considerations include the long-term vitality of wildlife habitats, rivers and lakes, forests and fisheries, plains and prairies, and the ocean, as well as air quality. To protect the environment, mitigating pollution and greenhouse gas emissions are at the top of the list. So is sustainable use of the earth's available natural resources, such as arable land and fresh water.

To reach your goal of being a conscious eater, ask yourself if you're optimizing at least one of these three factors with every food choice. Sometimes one will be enough—for instance, the deep satisfaction you should feel from knowing you made a delicious dinner for yourself and your family that was as healthy as could be. Other times, go for the trifecta. All in all, my hope in giving you this checklist is that it serves as your decision-making compass, helping you continuously gut-check the direction in which you're heading with your weekly grocery purchases, lunchtime routines, and restaurant orders.

Flavor is in the tongue of the taster, but it's a factor whose significance can't be overstated. That you actually *like* the way a food tastes is essential; otherwise you're unlikely to give a gnat's frass about how nutritious or great for others and the planet it is. Cost is critical, too. That you be able to *afford* the foods that meet the above criteria is also essential. Otherwise, again, who cares? Unfortunately, this country is plagued by huge inequities with respect to access to real, nourishing food—most alarmingly along lines of race, ethnicity, and socio-economic status. So too does food policy—from subsidies to special-interest groups—affect what we eat. This book does not intend to minimize the importance of taste, access, and policy, but it's simply not a guide for those domains.

This book is all about navigating the true luxury of abundance. With abundance comes a great privilege of having too many choices. Way too many. *How to Be a Conscious Eater* aims to help make your choices simpler, clearer, and ultimately more rewarding. We're all on a budget, so reading each section should help you allocate your grocery dollars toward the things that matter most to you.

What's good for you physically is almost always, inherently, without you even trying extra hard, good for the planet, too. Admittedly, this book skews slightly heavier toward environment and health than toward animal and social welfare. Not because the latter two aren't critically important. They are. It's just that the severity and urgency of the other two crises—climate change and obesity—require that we act so vigilantly to address them through our daily eating habits. Thankfully, if the intersection of human and environmental health is your north star, you most often will do good for others and animals while you're at it. I have woven in those direct considerations and emphasized when they should take first place on your list of things to care about (i.e., slavery in the seafood industry, factory farming and your meat choices).

A disclaimer: I'm giving advice as an author and journalist, not a medical practitioner. I'm not in a position to offer dietary recommendations tailored to your personal health profile. See the essay on page 236 about personalized nutrition, what we know and don't know, and when a one-size-fits-all approach to diet and health doesn't cut it. That said, there are general rules that apply to *most people*. Yes, talk to your doctor for any specific questions about your unique needs—especially if you have diabetes, prediabetes, cancer, heart disease, or allergies, or if you're pregnant or breastfeeding. But by and large this guide can help most people get through most food decisions with ease and assurance.

I have worked in the intersecting fields of American food culture and sustainable food systems, human health and social behavior for years. Meaning: I know a lot about what drives decisions about food, and how that sometimes differs from what *should* or *could* drive those decisions. In my day job at The Culinary Institute of America, I lead initiatives to help major US food-service companies make their menus healthier and better for the environment—from restaurants and fast food chains to K–12 school districts and campus dining programs. I moonlight as a food writer, most frequently for the *New York Times* Well section, where I debunk common food myths and answer readers' questions about what counts as "healthy." Also, I've spent my entire adult life as an aspiring conscious eater myself. My weekend hobby is (no joke) spending hours walking very, *very* slowly through the grocery store, studying products and labels. This book is based on all that experience combined.

More likely than not, you have at one point or another wondered about the nutritional calculus of coconut oil or the environmental footprint of soda cans, and upon consulting the Googleverse, found yourself marooned at the bottom of a dark, dank rabbit hole of twenty-seven different browser windows—and no clear answer. One of the main reasons for the twenty-seven different theories is that there is a lot of food tribalism telling you to ditch your practical side in favor of one all-consuming, character-defining dogma. To join whoever is making a pitch that their way is the best way and you'll have only yourself to blame if you ignore them. There has long been diet evangelism—for centuries, in fact, with all manner of weight-loss quackery—but today, with *digital* diet evangelism, it's more polarizing, moves at a faster pace, and is more effective, thanks to the sophistication of targeted advertising. It is utterly bewildering.

This guide is radically practical in the sense that being practical about eating is now more radical than following any number of super-restrictive diet regimens that historically would have been seen as radical. I'm talking about programs eliminating perfectly good food groups like legumes. With Whole 30, keto, paleo, gluten-free, intermittent fasting, and the like, food tribes have been on the rise. The percentage of American adults following a specific diet reached 38 percent in 2019 more than a third of the population—according to the International Food Information Council Foundation.

We are all suffering from one food myopia or another, and it's making for some seriously harmful habits. On the bright side, the situation suggests that once people get on a certain bandwagon, it completely colors how they relate to food. What if we could all jump aboard a sane bandwagon instead? I think we'd feel relieved. Clear-headed. Empowered.

PART 1

STUFF THAT COMES FROM THE GROUND

First, the bad news: Health-wise, our nation is in crisis. Maybe you're tired of hearing this. I sure am. We've been in this pickle for decades now: the prevalence and duration of the obesity epidemic going on multiple generations; crippling health care costs; compromised quality of life for millions of adults and children, many of whom are dying at ages younger than their parents and grandparents; and a serious threat to national security caused by a population unfit to serve in the armed forces. We're not alone, either: Globally, one in five deaths can be tied to poor diet.

Environment-wise, our planet is also in crisis. The newest research says that 2030 is the year by which climate change will significantly affect and even take more lives than it has in the past. Remember 2010? The Chilean miners, the BP oil spill, Wikileaks. Seems like a short time ago. It was ten years. That's how long we have to change things for the better before we see disasters that might include even more destructive episodes of extreme weather, heat and drought that put our health at risk, difficulty accessing clean drinking water, and eventually conflict between nations over who gets to use which natural resources to keep their people alive. And if the current standard operating procedures continue, the struggle of the people who grow our food—farmers and farmworkers—will become even more severe.

On the bright side, what would make the biggest difference for lowering our odds of diet-related disease is eating more healthy foods, as opposed to the usual finger-wagging to just cut the junk. Specifically, we're urged to consume more fruits, vegetables, healthy fats, nuts, seeds, legumes, and whole grains than we currently do. The conveniently great news is that what's good for the planet aligns almost *exactly* with what is good for our health.

Eating a plant-rich diet not only is the approach most tied to longevity and well-being but is also dubbed the fourth most effective climate-change-reversing solution. By no means necessarily vegan or vegetarian, what this means in practice is eating *mostly* plant-based foods. But not at the expense of flavor. Done right, eating lots of stuff from the ground can fill your belly and bring you joy.

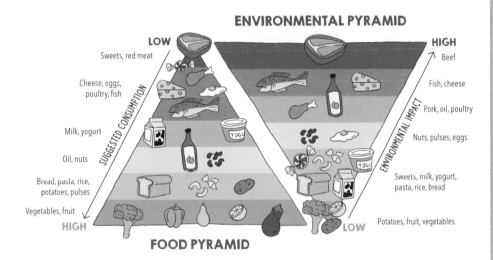

Source: Barilla Center for Food and Nutrition Foundation 2015

ALMONDS: HEALTH NUTS OR WATER HOGS?

Until about 2011, almonds were sitting pretty. Americans had finally gotten excited about regularly eating something genuinely good for them. Almond butter had penetrated the market to challenge peanut butter as the only game in town. But then, a scathing report brought the concept of a food's "water footprint" into the mainstream, and almonds became the poster child of foods that require an irresponsibly high amount of water. A water footprint is the amount of water involved in growing, processing, and delivering a food product to us. All together, the US agriculture industry sucks up about 80 percent of our country's available fresh water. In part because of climate change (drought, extreme temperatures, erratic rain), by the year 2025, two-thirds of the people on this planet could face water shortages. That's what's at stake here.

More than 80 percent of almonds eaten around the world are grown in California. One of the biggest gripes about the high toll on California's drought-stricken agriculture system is that two-thirds of the almonds grown are exported. This "virtual water" gets shipped abroad. Furthermore, wildlife comes under threat when water levels reach dangerously low levels, as when endangered king salmon in Northern California reportedly became imperiled by water being diverted to almond farms.

So, it was a big deal when we learned that it takes an entire gallon of water just to produce *one* almond. *Ouch.* Suddenly something long seen as a sign of a health-conscious eater was making shoppers think twice.

ALL OF THIS IS TRUE, BUT TWO CAVEATS ARE WARRANTED:

1   The high footprint is in part because, to date, most almond growers haven't been incentivized to use water efficiently. Almonds are an economic powerhouse for California, and my sense is that growers have not been motivated to be frugal because they either have historically had such cushy water rights or could afford to buy senior water rights from others by growing such a lucrative crop. Flood irrigation has long been the norm. But that's started to change post-exposé. Farmers have been shifting to more precise techniques like drip irrigation, resulting in a flat level of total water consumption as an industry—despite having doubled almond acreage in California over the past two decades.

2   Almonds get the most heat for high water use, but other foods require a lot, too. It takes 37 gallons to produce your cup of coffee. It takes 450 gallons to make just one bar of chocolate. And it takes a whopping 660 gallons to make a Whopper. The comparison with animal-based foods overall is especially unfavorable. Yet that big-picture message often gets lost in the fray.

It's not to say we turn a blind eye to almonds' thirsty ways, but we have to weigh that issue against the benefits of almonds, the broad appeal they have to Americans, and their availability to most people. In other words, we have to consider them in the context of other foods we're choosing between. Nutritionally, almonds (and pretty much all nuts) offer healthy fats, nutrients, and a good amount of protein. They can be high in calories, but worth it, especially for how full you often feel after eating just a handful. They're best consumed instead of less healthy snacks like chips, crackers, cookies, or candy. Consistently, large long-term studies—such as the

HOW MUCH WATER DOES IT TAKE?

Gallons of water required to produce one standard serving of the following food products:

HAMBURGER	660
CHOCOLATE BAR	450
4 OUNCES OF CHICKEN	117
1 GLASS OF MILK	55
1 EGG	53
1 AVOCADO	45
1 SLICE OF CHEESE	37
1 CUP OF COFFEE	37
1 GLASS OF WINE	32
HANDFUL OF ALMONDS	23
1 GLASS OF BEER	20
1 APPLE	18
1 SLICE OF BREAD	11
STRAWBERRIES	10
CARROTS	7
1 POTATO	7

Adventist Health Studies, the Iowa Women's Health Study, and the Nurses' Health Study—find that regular nut eaters have a lower likelihood of having a heart attack or developing heart disease. As much as a 30 to 50 percent lower chance, in fact. And a lower risk of type 2 diabetes. There just aren't that many foods out there with such a well-established body of evidence to support their being a regular fixture in our diets for long-term health outcomes.

With every food choice you make, ask yourself, *As opposed to what?* If we're talking about a handful of almonds versus a stick of string cheese, which wins? The handful of almonds has a lower water footprint. Almonds also win for health and carbon footprint. (The carbon footprint of a food is the amount of greenhouse gases, especially carbon dioxide, emitted to grow, process, and deliver it to us.) Or let's take breakfast. Almond butter toast instead of a bacon-and-egg breakfast sandwich? Almond butter toast across the board. In your coffee, almond milk's carbon footprint is about half that of dairy milk, according to an analysis by Planet Vision. Nutritionally, it depends on the brand and how each type of milk is made. Water-wise, almond milk wins over dairy (cows need a lot of water).

But of course there are plenty of other tasty nuts with comparable health benefits, great flavor, and a water footprint similar to or even lower than that of almonds. Walnuts and pistachios top the list. Peanuts are the lowest water users of all the nuts, and the most affordable.

As for how almonds affect others, don't overlook food allergies. Tree nuts (Brazil nuts, cashews, hazelnuts, pistachios, and walnuts, in addition to almonds) are one of the eight most common allergens in the United States.

2

WHY WATER BEATS ALL, AND TAP BEATS BOTTLE

Along time ago, around 1970, almost nobody paid to drink water. It was a ridiculous notion. Then someone figured out that, like everything else, if you add a snazzy label to it and maybe a few celebrity endorsements, people will buy. And buy we have. Bottled water is now a nearly $19 billion industry in the United States.

Now, to be clear, I *want* you to drink water. In fact, plain old water is by far the healthiest beverage to consume in copious amounts. Drinking water keeps your digestive system on track and can help you maintain a healthy weight because it fills you up. Water beats milk, soda, juice, energy drinks, and sports drinks for daily hydration. We can't live without water; we can live without Red Bull. (And I hear some people can even live without wine, those noble souls.) The point is, drink water. And drink it from the tap instead of bottled. Because:

* It's free.
* It's safe.
* It's better for the planet.
* It provides you with fluoride.

TO BREAK IT DOWN

Cost: We spend as much as 2,000 times more for a gallon of bottled water than for one from the tap. Two thousand times! That's according to a 2018 report by Food & Water Watch. Why waste your money for something that gets delivered to your kitchen for free? (OK, technically you pay for home tap water through your monthly water bill, but it's been estimated that this costs $0.004 per gallon. That's less than a penny for 16 cups of water. Practically free.) Reusable containers—whether a glass at home or a water bottle on the go—are the best way to hydrate, for both financial and environmental sustainability.

Safety: We have one of the best, most reliable public water systems in the world. Ninety percent of the time, your community water source in the United States meets or exceeds the federal water safety standards for contaminants (e.g., from agricultural runoff) and bacteria. If you're wondering if you're in the 10 percent whose doesn't, know that by law your water provider must deliver a consumer confidence report annually by mail. You can check online for it anytime through the Environmental Protection Agency. At least in theory. I tried actually doing this and, it being a government website, nothing worked as advertised. It was extremely confusing. Instead, contact your local utility directly for the report, or search your district in the Environmental Working Group's more user-friendly website. The point is, if you have concerns about the safety of your home tap water, get peace of mind by having it tested. The Food & Water Watch report also points out that tap water is subjected to more rigorous safety testing than bottled water—something most people don't realize. I didn't.

Now, there are certainly exceptions to the assumed safety of tap water in the United States. In Flint, Michigan, most notably, residents suffered from devastating and scandalous lead contamination. Though the situation has since improved, any residents who are still waiting for their lead pipes to be replaced have good reason to remain wary of water from their sinks. As with anyone who has concerns, Flint residents have been encouraged to get their water tested and use a filter.

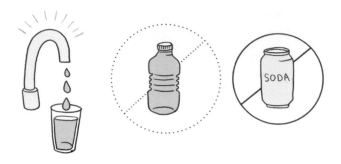

What about health? If we assume that bottled water is displacing other worse beverages like soda, that's progress. And in fact, since the early 2000s, the downward trend of soda sales has coincided with the upward trend of bottled water sales. In a major tipping point, in 2016 Americans bought more bottled water than bottled soda. Something to celebrate, no? The trouble is the false premise of the marketing: Manufacturers position it as a healthy alternative to soda (which it is). Except that choosing bottled water should be compared with choosing tap water. In that light, it's a bamboozling, environmentally worse, health-wise-neutral, far more expensive alternative.

The planet: It takes a lot of resources to make and ship bottled water (more in Part 3 on the environmental harms of churning through so many single-use plastics). From there, reports vary widely about recycling rates, from as low as about 17 percent to a high of only about 54 percent. The rest winds up in landfills, polluting lakes, or adding to the Great Pacific Garbage Patch. That's a 600,000-square-mile patch of floating garbage, made up of nearly two trillion pieces of plastic floating between California and Hawaii. Studies estimate that over fifty billion plastic bottles of water get consumed each year in the United States—more than twice the amount consumed in 2000. The average family of four now goes through an entire case a week.

Fluoridation: Ignore the fearmongering chatter, because the American Dental Association, Centers for Disease Control and Prevention (CDC), and other credible health officials agree that fluoridated tap water is good for long-term oral health. Considered one of the greatest public health achievements of the past century, it means you get to spend less time in the dentist's office having your teeth drilled.

REASONS TO THINK TWICE BEFORE DRINKING YOUR TAP WATER

You rely on a private well instead of public supply. This is roughly 10 percent of Americans. Private wells aren't regulated by the EPA's Safe Drinking Water Act standards, so you are encouraged to test the water from yours annually for bacteria, other contaminants like heavy metals, and pH levels.

You are pregnant or have young kids. The possibility of lead contamination is the main exception to the clear, obvious, unequivocal advantage of tap water over bottled. The vast majority of utilities stopped using lead lines in the 1980s, but between approximately six million and twenty-two million Americans still get their tap water via lead pipes, which may not appear in your citywide water report. Lead exposure, especially for kids, is a serious matter. Elevated lead levels affect cognitive development and behavior. So those who are pregnant or have young kids are encouraged to test their own water. Call the EPA's safe drinking water hotline (800-426-4791) or your local water utility to find the form and a lab where you can send a sample from your faucet. I did this myself through the San Francisco Public Utilities Commission and it worked great. They mailed me an empty testing bottle, which I filled from my kitchen sink, and then I called them to come pick it up from my doorstep. A few weeks later I received notice from the lab that my water's lead levels were quite safe. It cost $25, which was a lot, but it was well worth it for the peace of mind—and the savings—to continue drinking my tap water.

You checked your water district's safety report and it got a bad score. If you think your water may be cause for concern, once you know the status of your tap water, consider buying a filter certified by NSF International, an organization that helps consumers with issues related to the health and safety of food, water, and various products. Different tap water filters remove different contaminants, and they range from "point-of-use" options like pitchers and contraptions you install under the sink to treatment systems for your whole house. See more information at *nsf.org*.

THE FIZZY FIX

Now, if it's bubbles you're after, buy a home carbonator, such as SodaStream, and make your own sparkling water. (*Sparkling water* is the umbrella term for carbonated water, including naturally carbonated sparkling mineral water and artificially carbonated seltzer and club soda.) It'll sure save you money. Sparkling water companies sell approximately 800 million gallons, or $8.5 billion worth, in the United States each year. LaCroix (Nasdaq symbol FIZZ) is even traded on the stock market.

Despite persistent rumors, bubbles are not bad for you. It's just pressurized carbon dioxide. Your bone density and teeth are safe. And, if you make your own effervescence, you don't have to worry about whether the manufacturer snuck in added sweeteners or other additives.

THE BEST PRODUCE IS THE KIND YOU EAT

O f all the things you could possibly do for your health, eating more fruits and vegetables is far and away one of the best. It's that simple.

You'll want to aim for at least five servings a day and a delicious diversity. Eating enough veggies is especially important. Fortunately, a serving is not as big as you may think—you can easily have two or three in one sitting. If they can be organic, great. If they can be seasonal and regional, great. The primary thing is to eat them.

HOW MUCH IS A SERVING?

Here are some examples of a serving of fruit and a serving of vegetables. Aim for five a day total.

ONE MEDIUM FRUIT

RAW LEAFY VEGETABLES

FRESH, FROZEN, OR CANNED FRUIT

FRESH, FROZEN, OR CANNED VEGETABLES

Adapted from the American Heart Association

WHY ORGANIC IS BETTER, WHEN YOU CAN AFFORD IT

Being a conscious eater means of course that you care not only about your own health and that of your family but also about the impact of your food choices on others and the planet. Dozens of different third-party certifications are used on food products, so depending on your budget and the things you care most about supporting, certain ones may be worth the extra cost. The US Department of Agriculture (USDA)'s organic label is arguably the most rigorously backed certification on the market. It's not perfect, but it checks a lot of boxes.

WHAT'S AT STAKE FOR THE PLANET

According to the USDA, the practices that distinguish organic agriculture include "maintaining or enhancing soil and water quality; conserving wetlands, woodlands, and wildlife; and avoiding use of synthetic fertilizers, sewage sludge, irradiation, and genetic engineering." Organic processes "contribute to soil, crop and livestock nutrition, pest and weed management, attainment of production goals, and conservation of biological diversity." Among a portfolio of practices, managing pests and weeds is a major difference between conventional and organic production methods, so pesticides, insecticides, and herbicides are top-of-mind considerations in deciding between the two. Conventional industrial agriculture is characterized by maximizing the yield of crops above all else—doing so through energy-intensive farming practices and synthetic chemicals as fertilizers, at the expense of the surrounding environment. By contrast, rather than using chemicals with abandon, organic farmers first work to prevent and avoid pests, insects, and weeds and then, if need be, suppress them through approved substances. As a general rule, substances that are naturally derived are allowed, whereas synthetic substances are prohibited, though there are exceptions in both directions. Not that being made by humans automatically makes something bad, but it's worth noting that conventional agriculture has at its disposal at least 900 approved synthetic pesticides, whereas organic agriculture has only 25. All told, organic farms host more biodiversity (from bees to butterflies), release fewer greenhouse gases into the air, and enhance the quality of their soil and water. Yields vary but can certainly be less than non-organic. This can lead to the need for more farmland to grow the same amount of food, which may be a potential drawback.

WHAT'S AT STAKE FOR OTHERS

Organically grown produce means significantly less exposure to pesticides, and therefore far lower risk of the long-term reproductive, cognitive, or cancer-related health problems that have been tied to the chemicals. The health problems associated with certain toxic agrochemicals are especially concerning for farmworkers, whose exposure is higher and more direct than that of consumers, often through skin contact or breathing the chemicals, rather than by ingesting food with chemical residues.

The same goes for rural communities that may be exposed because of pesticide drift, which occurs when chemicals get carried through the air after being sprayed on a given plot. This issue disproportionately affects low-income communities of color, who often lack the political capital to earn the environmental justice protections they deserve.

Economic development—boosting rural communities and helping to lift farmers living on the margins out of poverty—

may be another benefit of supporting organic practices. Some research suggests that because farmers earn a premium on organically grown food, it provides higher incomes to help run small- or medium-sized family farms. By one estimate, organic farmers earn about 35 percent more than conventional farmers, at least those in North America, Europe, and India. That said, actual wages and labor conditions for farmworkers are by no means necessarily any better under organic standards. On farms of all types, some alarming conditions have been reported, such as backbreaking repetitive motions, heat exhaustion and dehydration, forced labor, withheld pay, and lack of breaks. For assurance of fair labor practices, a handful of farms from California to Florida and New York have earned Food Justice Certification from the Agricultural Justice Project. The certification earns Consumer Reports' "highly meaningful" designation; see *greenerchoices.org*.

WHAT'S AT STAKE FOR YOUR OWN HEALTH

Overall, the risks to human health are fairly low from most pesticide residues, or so it appears thus far, and at least according to the USDA and the EPA. That said, certain pesticides are more hazardous than others.

* The type of chemicals that appear to be the most toxic are called organophosphates. A 2016 investigation by the EPA led to the conclusion that one such chemical, chlorpyrifos—which is commonly used on more than fifty crops, from broccoli and cauliflower to apples and oranges, and has been linked to acute illness among farmworkers and rural residents exposed to it, and to more severe long-term problems for babies and children, such as lower IQ, low birth weight, and developmental delays—was not safe and should be banned. But that ban has since been rejected. It remains to be seen what happens policy-wise, but regardless, we'll

all want to steer clear of it. (See the shopping tips in the next essay.) Thankfully, use of these chemicals has already declined, so their prevalence is not as high as it once was.

* The most widely used herbicide in conventional agriculture is called glyphosate. In 2015, it was dubbed a probable human carcinogen by the International Agency on Cancer Research. More recently, in a very public court case against Monsanto, a giant chemical company that produces herbicides containing glyphosate (Roundup and Ranger Pro are the trade names), a San Francisco groundskeeper won nearly $300 million by demonstrating that exposure to these chemicals from spraying them in his job significantly contributed to his life-threatening non-Hodgkin's lymphoma.

* When it comes to exposure through food, the people at highest risk are women and men trying to conceive, pregnant women, and children. A few studies suggest some compromised fertility, and in utero or early childhood exposure to organophosphates has been associated with damage to the brain and nervous systems, as well as Attention-Deficit/Hyperactivity Disorder (ADHD).

There's a lot we don't know yet about pesticides and health. This is especially true of the long-term, cumulative effects of exposure to residues in food even if they're present at low levels at a given time. Plus, questions abound from many environmental groups and farmworker advocacy groups about the synergistic effects of pesticides used together, and how that could affect health risks. Given the historical track record in the United States of finding out only years later that things long allowed in the food supply are bad for us, I argue for the better-safe-than-sorry approach—while keeping a level head. Read on to see what that means in practice.

5

RADICALLY PRACTICAL TIPS FOR BUYING PRODUCE

I n the spirit of being a conscious eater while making your meals as satisfying and downright joyful for yourself as possible, here are my top tips for buying produce you can feel good about:

Just eat them. Only once you've found a way to afford, access, and feed yourself and your family sufficient servings of fruits and vegetables should you worry about anything else. Eating at least five servings a day is far and away the number one priority.

Be strategic on organic. It's unrealistic for most of us to have the budget to buy organic everything. But if you'd like to choose some organic produce and want to know where you get the most bang for your buck, follow the Environmental Working Group's Dirty Dozen and Clean Fifteen. The Dirty Dozen lists the types of produce with the highest levels of pesticide residue. Strawberries and spinach are at the top of the list, along with apples, grapes, tomatoes, bell peppers, and more. As a general rule, if you eat the skin, opt for organic. If not, and it has a peel instead—bananas, avocados, oranges, and so on— buying organic is less important. The Clean Fifteen are the produce categories with the lowest levels of pesticide residue. The list includes avocados and sweet corn as the cleanest, along with asparagus, eggplant, cauliflower, pineapples, and more. Read more at *ewg.org*.

THE EWG'S DIRTY DOZEN

If you are able, it's a good idea to buy organic versions of these foods that have the highest levels of pesticide residue.

STRAWBERRIES

PEACHES

TOMATOES

GRAPES

APPLES

SPINACH

PEARS

CHERRIES

CELERY

POTATOES

NECTARINES

KALE

Mothers, babies, children. The American Academy of Pediatrics recommends that if you're pregnant or have young children, wash all fruits and vegetables and buy organic produce when possible to minimize exposure to pesticide residues. You're also encouraged to choose fresh or frozen produce to minimize exposure to BPA, a harmful plastic that lines many metal cans, including some canned fruits and vegetables.

Eat seasonally. Why? You get peak flavor. If you're introducing a new fruit or vegetable to a kid or trying to get yourself or your partner to like something, the chances it will stick are higher if your trials are with the best possible version of that thing. The same goes for preparation: A mushy, boiled Brussels sprout doesn't have a fraction of the crave-worthiness of a crispy, roasted one.

Diversify. The vast majority of the food we eat—75 percent—comes from a skimpy twelve types of plants and five species of animals. What a missed opportunity! By eating with the seasons or simply branching out from your go-to ingredients, you experience more types of flavors, nutrients, textures, and pairings with other foods over the course of the year. Doing so can also greatly expand your cooking, as different types of foods will lend themselves to different dishes. Both the better flavor and the thrill of discovery create a positive feedback loop for you and your family: Tried an interesting new vegetable (Romanesco cauliflower! Celery root! Tomatillo!) → Tasted better than expected → Likely to eat it again. And this, in turn, can go a long way toward a lifelong habit of reaching those five servings a day.

Eat regionally. Regional eating includes focusing on produce from as close as your backyard to as far as the same general climate as your home state—the Pacific Northwest, for example. Transportation makes up a mere 11 percent of the greenhouse gas (GHG) emissions of food production, so honoring the spirit of "locally sourced" need not mean sticking to items from within a certain radius of your home. A regional approach is also a more realistic and actionable way of eating than strict locavorism. Here's what I mean:

* It expands your options while still giving you connection to place. This allows you to use your grocery dollars to support surrounding economies—from farmers to farmworkers, distributors to processors.

* Again, as with seasonal produce, the flavor will likely be higher. Regionally sourced produce often arrives to you fresher. And, with long-term storage and shipping removed from the equation, fruits and vegetables from nearby are given the chance to fully ripen in the field.

* You get to know the people behind your food. As the number of farmers has dramatically declined, and more and more of us live in cities, we've become disconnected from not only how food is grown but who grows it. Talking to the growers behind your food (such as by buying your produce from farmers' markets) allows you to learn about their land and family history and understand how their produce gets, well, produced. There are major financial burdens to converting to organic; some farms are effectively organic, or even regenerative or biodynamic, but don't get certified. Foods don't have to be certified organic to have been grown using safe, sustainable, responsible practices.

DO WE REALLY NEED TO WASH FRESH PRODUCE BEFORE EATING IT?

Yes. For two reasons:

1 **AVOID FOOD POISONING.** According to the CDC, germs on fresh produce are responsible for nearly half of all foodborne illnesses. Harmful bacteria can catch a ride on your apple or your carrots or your head of lettuce, whether from the farm, during storage, or from fellow shoppers feeling them up before the items land in your grocery basket. Ever had a foodborne illness like norovirus? It wipes you out for days. Not fun.

2 **REMOVE PESTICIDE RESIDUE.** This is, of course, particularly relevant for produce that's not organic.

Rinse produce right before you're going to eat it. Don't wash and then refrigerate, because bacteria thrive in moisture. Plain running water is best, with a gentle rub from your freshly washed hands. Dry it with a clean cloth or paper towel. There is no need to wash prewashed items like bagged salad greens.

6

TOP 5 WAYS TO WASTE LESS FOOD AT HOME

All told, more than 30 percent of all the food produced around the world never gets eaten. In the United States, it's 40 percent. After going to all the trouble to produce food, we're actually sending it to landfills. Food scraps contribute more volume to landfill than anything else. So, of all the things you can possibly do to lower your carbon footprint, wasting less food is by far one of the most effective. (The other is eating less red meat.)

At the same time, 40 million Americans go hungry every day. The problem isn't producing enough food. In countries like the United States, the biggest issue is retailer and consumer tendencies, from over-buying and over-portioning to not being OK with "running out" of certain things in home pantries or on grocery shelves. Confusing "best by" dates don't do us any favors. If we could just distribute one-third of the food that goes uneaten, it would feed all the food-insecure Americans who desperately need it.

The reason you're reading about this issue in the section on stuff that comes from the ground is that globally the two food categories most likely to be wasted are (1) fruits and vegetables and (2) roots and tubers. Some of our most nutritious crops—squandered! Yes, even in the United States, some food waste occurs on the farm or on its way to us: Produce got too ripe or was deemed not pretty enough or not uniform enough in size to be sold (so-called "ugly produce"). But nearly half of the problem is on us. (Google "Your Plan, Your Planet," a fun interactive tool for wasting less food.) For example, in North America and Oceania alone, approximately 5.8 million tons of roots and tubers are wasted *just at the consumption stage.* That's according to the Food and Agriculture Organization of the United Nations, and it's the equivalent of 1 billion bags of potatoes. Picture raw potatoes you forgot about in your kitchen pantry, trays of excess fries tossed after lunch in a school cafeteria, or all those breakfast potatoes left uneaten at brunch.

At home, there are effective steps you and your family can take to waste less food. Dana Gunders, a former senior scientist at the Natural Resources Defense Council, authored a fantastic book called the *Waste-Free Kitchen Handbook.* Her general advice is to apply the waste management mantra "Reduce, Reuse, Recycle" to food.

TOP 5 WAYS TO WASTE LESS FOOD AT HOME

1   ALWAYS USE A SHOPPING LIST. Making a list before grocery shopping is obvious, simple, and highly effective. Yet surprisingly few people use one. Those who do are less likely to succumb to impulse buys. Also, before you check out at the register, take a moment to review every item in your cart and make sure you have a plan for using each one.

2   OF ALL THE THINGS NOT TO WASTE, RED MEAT IS THE MOST IMPORTANT. Not all food waste has the same impact on the planet. Tossing an uneaten hamburger wastes the water equivalent of taking a ninety-minute shower. For a tomato, it's more like four or five minutes. So, in terms of lowering your carbon and water footprints—especially if eating less red meat feels like a tough lifestyle adjustment—not wasting the red meat you do purchase is a great place to start. What counts as red meat? Meat from mammals, which in the United States is usually beef, pork, and lamb. Common

MORE THAN 30 PERCENT OF
ALL THE FOOD PRODUCED
AROUND THE WORLD
NEVER GETS EATEN.
IN THE UNITED STATES,
IT'S 40 PERCENT.

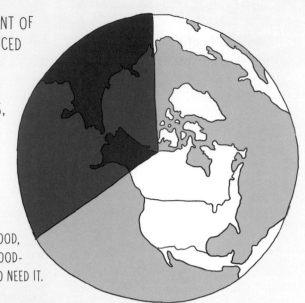

AT THE SAME TIME,
40 MILLION AMERICANS
GO HUNGRY EVERY DAY.
IF WE DISTRIBUTED ONE-
THIRD OF OUR UNEATEN FOOD,
IT WOULD FEED ALL THE FOOD-
INSECURE AMERICANS WHO NEED IT.

IN NORTH AMERICA AND OCEANIA, ABOUT 5.8 MILLION TONS OF
ROOTS AND TUBERS ARE WASTED *JUST AT THE CONSUMPTION
STAGE*—EQUAL TO 1 BILLION BAGS OF POTATOES.

examples of things not to waste range from burgers you grill in the backyard to a supermarket deli sandwich you bring home to a broccoli beef stir-fry from your take-out order.

3   LOVE YOUR LEFTOVERS. Like produce, leftovers are one of the most commonly wasted types of food. This is one of several examples of how reducing food waste at home actually starts away from home: When you're out, think before you order, aiming for no leftovers. If you have any, eat or freeze them within four days. Designate a section of the refrigerator as "eat this first." Use certain days of the week to focus on your leftovers—Stir-Fry Fridays, say, or Waste-Less Wednesdays.

4   MAKE FOOD VISIBLE. Fruits and vegetables are usually wasted because they spoil or get moldy. Make sure they don't get pushed to the back of the fridge or buried in the crisper, or get dusty in a bowl on the table. Keep them where you'll see them, and keep them looking ready to eat.

5   POP IT IN THE FREEZER. According to Gunders, you can freeze just about anything, including bread (best if you slice it), cheese (best if you shred it), and even milk and eggs (best if you scramble them raw out of their shells first).

7

BEANS, THE HUMBLE HEROES

O f all the items in the American grocery store, I'd argue that legumes are the Clark Kents: often ignored, yet harboring hidden superpowers. We're talking lentils, peanuts, peas, and the many stripes of beans, from black beans and kidney beans to soybeans and garbanzo beans (aka chickpeas). These low-key seeds are actually little heroes. Celebrated in cultures and cuisines all around the world, and nutritional powerhouses in their own right—full of fiber, plant protein, and nutrients, all at a small caloric price point—legumes are especially stars on the sustainability field.

What's so magical about them? First and foremost, nitrogen fixation. Not a household term, I know. Atmospheric nitrogen is the nitrogen that's in the air—accounting for 78 percent of the air we breathe. Meaning there's lots of it. By contrast, nitrogen available to plants is harder to come by: They can't absorb it directly from the air. That's where legumes come in. They're a converter of sorts, pulling nitrogen from the air and fixing it, or transforming it, into a form that helps plants grow. They do this by pumping nitrogen into the soil through their roots, thanks to a unique type of microbe that takes up residence there. The legume's roots essentially feed and house those microbes in an unusually friendly tenant-landlord relationship.

Because nitrogen is so important for producing healthy crops, synthetic nitrogen fertilizers are often used in farming, but legumes don't require that fertilizer. Nitrogen fixing boosts soil health, which can boost yields. And, most altruistically of all, because of the way legumes enrich the soil around them, they actually lower the greenhouse gas emissions of crops planted there *after they are gone*. Like a beachgoer who cleans up not just her own picnic spot but the sand surrounding her area, legumes are pros at paying it forward. This feature makes the plant proteins a great option for farmers practicing crop rotation on their farmland, alternating them between grains (such as wheat or barley) or seeds (such as canola or flax).

IF YOU'RE NOT CONVINCED THAT NITROGEN FIXING IS ENOUGH TO EARN LEGUMES A PLACE IN YOUR HOUSEHOLD GROCERY ROTATION, CONSIDER THESE OTHER BENEFITS:

* They win the prize for lowest environmental footprint of any major protein source. Per 100 grams of protein, lentils emit just 1 measly kilogram of greenhouse gases. For dry beans, the number is only 2.3 kg. Compare that to 3.8 for eggs, 9.6 for beef, and 14.1 for lamb. Per serving produced, lentils and dry beans need only 45 and 58 gallons of water, respectively (assuming standard 1-ounce servings). Compare that with 124 and 320 gallons for pork and

PROTEIN FOOTPRINTS

Here's how common foods stack up in terms of greenhouse gas emissions per gram of protein.

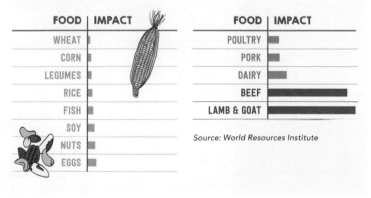

FOOD	IMPACT		FOOD	IMPACT
WHEAT			POULTRY	
CORN			PORK	
LEGUMES			DAIRY	
RICE			BEEF	
FISH			LAMB & GOAT	
SOY				
NUTS				
EGGS				

Source: World Resources Institute

beef, respectively (assuming standard 3-ounce servings). Because of these low water needs, legumes can be a critical protein source for people living in dry or hot parts of the world.

* Generally speaking, whether canned or dry, legumes are extremely affordable.

* Because they're central to so many global cuisines, a huge variety of flavorful dishes is waiting to be discovered. And of those cuisines, many are from parts of the world whose populations tend to live the longest, from the Mediterranean (chickpeas and white beans) to Japan (tofu and miso). Coincidence? I think not.

So, when you compare the worldwide population benefits to the hype from the Whole 30 crowd or others banishing legumes from their lips, it's clear that for the majority of eaters, the upsides far outweigh the downsides. Despite much talk about inflammation and anti-inflammatory diets, research does not support claims that legumes (or whole grains or nightshade vegetables, like eggplant and peppers, for that matter) increase inflammation. Plus, although many people avoid legumes because their bodies aren't used to that much fiber, experts say that your stomach adjusts after just a few weeks of incorporating them into your diet.

IMPORTANT EXCEPTION: Peanut allergies can be lethal. And allergies have been on the rise, especially among children. When hosting a party or bringing a dish to a potluck, keep in mind that what can be a nutritious, delicious food for most people can be life-threatening for the roughly 1 percent of Americans who are allergic.

8

THE GLORY OF
WHOLE GRAINS

I f there's one thing you will learn in this book, it's that there is no one food or even one food group that unlocks the gate to lifelong health. That said, just as lentils are our little environmental hotshots, whole grains are our unsung health heroes. Eating whole grains has been linked to a crazy number of good health outcomes: As part of a healthy diet, eating lots of whole grains has been tied to a lower risk of heart disease, type 2 diabetes, obesity, and, oh, overall chance of death.

Whole grains are much more accessible than most people think. You're probably eating many of them already. They're in:

popcorn, including cheddar popcorn and kettle corn // corn tortillas // tortilla chips from corn // oatmeal cookies // granola bars // brown rice // soba noodles from buckwheat

What makes a grain whole? And does that make other grains ... empty? Come to think of it, yes. Nutritionally, that is.

KEY TERMS FOR UNDERSTANDING THE GLORY OF WHOLE GRAINS

Whole grains are made of three main components: the bran, the germ, and the endosperm. Whole grains retain all three components when eaten—meaning they are eaten intact or are milled in a way that retains these parts. This matters because the germ and the bran are by far the most nutritious parts. They offer dietary fiber, healthy fats, protein, antioxidants, and many vitamins and minerals. Fiber is important for maintaining healthy gut bacteria as well as overall digestive health, so

SERVINGS OF WHOLE GRAINS

Here are a few examples and portion sizes. Aim for three servings a day.

| 1 SLICE OF WHOLE-GRAIN BREAD | ½ CUP OF OATMEAL | ½ CUP OF COOKED BROWN RICE |

inadequate intake can lead to constipation and other not-fun issues in the lavatory. The endosperm is mainly just starch. Whole grains include both intact grains (such as wheat berries) and grains ground into flour (such as whole-wheat bread).

Intact grains: Not only do they retain all three parts, but the grain kernels themselves are sold intact. This means no processing except to clean the kernels and make them edible—no steaming, milling, or pulverizing.

Refined grains: The bran and germ have been removed from refined grains. This gives flour a longer shelf life and finer texture, but the fiber and most of the nutrients get removed in the process. Common examples of refined grains are white rice, white flour, and the many products made from white flour—from white bread and bagels to cookies and cakes.

Enriched grains: They sound promising, but they're a far cry from whole grains. It seems ludicrous, but this is really what happens: Manufacturers first strip out the healthiest assets of the grain—the germ and the bran—to improve shelf life or get that fine texture. Then they add back in *some* of the nutrients that were originally in those components. They slap a label on the box of the now highly processed product to tout the nutrient content and position it as a value-added item. You're much better off buying the product whose nutritional mojo hasn't been removed in the first place.

Make sure *at least half* of the total grains you eat each day are whole grains. That's the recommendation of the Dietary Guidelines for Americans. Aim for 48 grams of whole grains per day, or three servings. Common examples of a serving are a slice of 100 percent whole-grain bread, a half cup of oatmeal, or a half cup of cooked brown rice. According to the Whole Grains Council, nearly half of us don't eat whole grains at all.

I say go for the gusto and make whole grains your default, aiming to have them account for three-fourths or more of your total grains. Save those occasions when you eat refined grains for something really worth it—a phenomenal fresh-baked naan, say, or perfectly chewy sushi rice, or a croissant that's light as air. Thankfully, delicious whole-grain options are widely available, in a variety of forms and cuisine types, accessible to most shoppers, at relatively reasonable prices. (A giant tub of rolled oats is about $4, for an average of 13 cents per serving. Even if you get elaborate with berries or banana or chia or peanut butter or walnuts or raisins, you're looking at maybe $0.75 to $1.25 per breakfast.)

Notes on oats: Regular, or old-fashioned, oats come from steaming and rolling the oat kernel, or groat, into flat flakes. These are the middle-of-the-pack type of oatmeal in terms of processing, texture, and cook time. Steel-cut are the least processed, since the oat kernel is sliced into just a few pieces so that water can permeate and cook them. Quick, or instant, oats are also rolled but into thinner flakes and steamed longer. All three types of unsweetened oats are essentially the same nutritionally, and much better than the sugary instant packets; go for whichever you like the texture of, and add fruit, nuts, and other flavors yourself.

IF WHOLE GRAINS ARE SO GREAT, WHY DON'T WE EAT MORE OF THEM?

* POINT: With demand far in favor of white flour in recent generations, the most common types of wheat in the United States have been bred for easy milling into refined flour and long shelf life. As author Michael Pollan describes in his book *Cooked*, the reasons for this are that the texture of bran, even when milled, keeps it from getting as light and airy as many people like in their baked goods, not to mention that bran is rather bitter compared with refined flour's sweetness; also, the germ's healthy fats make it "unstable," meaning it goes rancid when exposed to air, so the resulting flour doesn't last that long. When eaten as whole-wheat bread or pasta, many flours don't offer much in terms of texture or flavor. COUNTERPOINT: After realizations that whole-grain flours require different techniques to bring out their best, whole-grain baking has come a long way. It's now easier to find great-tasting whole-wheat breads, cereals, and baked goods. Plus, several producers—from Community Grains in California and Bob's Red Mill in Oregon to Anson Mills in South Carolina—are breeding and milling wheat in ways better suited to eating it as whole-wheat flour. For now, these products are usually more expensive and a bit harder to find in stores, but over time, their world-of-difference flavor will no doubt bring them into widespread supply.

* POINT: Whole grains take longer to cook than similar refined versions. Brown rice takes about three times as long as white rice, for instance; it depends on the brand, but whole-wheat pasta can take an extra few minutes; and oatmeal takes longer to make than pouring cereal into a bowl. These scenarios are all pretty frustrating if you've got a

hangry partner waiting on dinner or screaming kids who need shoving out the door for school. COUNTERPOINT: Know there are good reasons why you're spending an extra few minutes. Brown rice is brown because it still has the bran; that's also what gives it and other tasty intact grains like farro a wonderful nutty flavor. To get around the time crunch, many people find that batch-cooking intact grains on Sundays does the trick. That way you can use them in meals throughout the week. Overnight oats are another antidote to the morning mayhem.

* POINT: Whole grains provide carbohydrates. People with diabetes or prediabetes need to be careful about how many carbs they eat. And low-carb diets were/are/will always be a thing. COUNTERPOINT: Not all carbohydrates are created equal. Yes, potato chips, white rice, sugary beverages, refined-flour pastries and cakes, and similar ultra-processed foods aren't worth the carb intake because of how they spike blood sugar, which overstimulates the pancreas, which leads to insulin resistance, which increases the risk of type 2 diabetes. So, although most people can and should enjoy whole-grain foods, those with prediabetes or diabetes need to be extra vigilant in reading labels and spending their carbohydrate budget carefully. You can't tell from the Nutrition Facts panel how many whole-grains servings are in a product, so check for the Whole Grains Council's stamp and the ingredients list to see if the first ingredient (or even only ingredient) is a whole grain—such as quinoa, brown rice, whole-wheat flour, and so on.

THE RUNDOWN ON WHOLE-GRAINS LABELS

To check the whole-grains content of packaged foods, I recommend looking for one of the stamps from the Whole Grains Council.

ONES TO PAY ATTENTION TO:

100% Whole Grain: Of the grain in the product, all of it is whole grain. Must have a minimum of 16 grams per serving, which is equivalent to one serving of whole grains.

50%+ Whole Grain: Of the grain in the product, at least half is whole grain. Must have a minimum of 8 grams per serving, equivalent to a half serving of whole grains.

Whole Grain: Of the grain in the product, less than half is whole grain. The most basic stamp, it also must provide at least 8 grams of whole grains per serving, but proportionally it might be more refined grain than whole.

ONES TO IGNORE:

Multigrain: Too hard to tell. It could mean a mix of whole grains, a mix of refined grains, or a mix of some number of each, but since the label alone doesn't indicate one way or another, it's best not to make much of this one.

Made with Whole Grain: Again, too ambiguous. This label doesn't set any threshold for how much of the grain is whole, so it could be just trace amounts.

9

TIPS FOR ENJOYING GRAINS

Buy local. Until a little over 100 years ago when industrial agriculture started to take over, farmers would bring their grain to a community mill. But local grain economies have largely disappeared as production has instead become consolidated in just a few parts of the country. Recently, however, stone milling techniques have made a comeback across the United States. You can support local farmers while contributing to local economies through the range of players involved, from millers to bakers. A resource for finding farms, mills, and malt houses in your area is the Local Grains Map at *wholegrainscouncil.org.*

Buy from manufacturers whose growing and milling practices are aligned with your values. Food producers labeled as B Corporations mean the businesses meet a high standard of verified social and environmental performance, public transparency, and legal accountability to balance profit and purpose. You can search the B Corp website (*bcorporation.net*) for manufacturers of whole-grain products. For the ultimate traceability, some manufacturers tell you the specific farming practices, water use, milling details, and harvest date and location of the exact plot of land where the wheat in your box of pasta or the corn in your bag of popcorn was grown.

Taste the rainbow. Yes, common whole-wheat bread and cheddar popcorn are easy ways to up your whole-grains intake, but there's an exciting range of lesser-known options. The Whole Grains Council's website lists over twenty types of whole grains in an "A to Z" resource, from ones milled into flours to those best cooked intact. There are also stories behind the different types of seeds. Ensuring the genetic diversity of our food supply is critical. You know the Irish Potato Famine? That's what happens when a population relies on just a few varieties of crops and then one bad, disease-causing pathogen wipes out the entire supply. This concern is only heightened by climate change, which has been affecting everything from the effectiveness of farmers' usual pesticide arsenal to weather patterns. To help create demand for more diversity, not to mention enjoy higher nutritional value than modern grains, you can exercise "seed stewardship" by buying products made from landrace, heirloom, and ancient grains.

* LANDRACE: These are grains that are uniquely suited to the climate and environment of certain regions, and hence have inspired certain iconic cuisine elements in those areas. Examples include White Sonora wheat from the American Southwest (ideal for making flour tortillas), Red Fife wheat from the central plains of Canada (ideal for making bread), and durum wheat in the Mediterranean (ideal for making pasta).

* HEIRLOOM AND ANCIENT: Heirloom grains are grown from seeds passed down from generation to generation, without any modification. Ancient grains are essentially super-heirloom (my term, not a technical term), meaning they date back millennia. Examples include amaranth, einkorn, emmer/farro, millet, quinoa, sorghum, spelt, and teff.

These attributes lend unique color, shape, and flavor beyond the typical grains most of us eat. Landrace, heirloom, and ancient grains can cost a bit more, but if you can afford it, the flavor is usually worth it. You'll be floored by the variety

WHAT'S SO GREAT ABOUT ANCIENT GRAINS?

From amaranth to einkorn, black barley to blue corn, farro to millet, quinoa to sorghum, spelt to teff, these are grains that have been underappreciated in Western supply chains. They are heirloom varieties of more common grains, or they're grains that have mostly stayed the same over at least the past century, if not longer. (More common grains like modern wheat, corn, and rice, on the other hand, are continuously bred or even genetically modified.) Ancient grains were first grown 5,000 to 10,000 years ago, right when the whole agriculture game was first kicking off. And on the whole, they are more nutritious. People's lives depended on their nutritional value, and generation after generation, the seeds were saved by hand and replanted to ensure the food supply. They were also valued because they could be grown in drought-intensive regions, something that makes them all the more relevant today amid warming global temperatures. Ancient grains tend to require less water, pesticides, and fertilizers, and they are sturdier in the face of sub-optimal soil and extreme weather. Millet, for example, has the lowest water needs of all the grains and thrives in Africa. Teff does particularly well in drought conditions. Primarily because their seeds yield a fraction of their modern counterparts, though, they fell out of favor with the rise of our industrialized food system; we need to feed a growing global population, after all. But their revival is welcome for the many reasons described—from superior nutrition and flavor to agricultural hardiness.

available from purveyors like Bob's Red Mill and Hayden Flour Mills.

Mill it yourself. The taste of fresh-milled whole-grain flour is an experience in itself. Often we consider grains to be merely vehicles for other flavors (jam on toast, sauce on pasta), but we're missing out on the inherent taste that many of these little guys have to offer. KoMo mills, distributed by Pleasant Hill Grain, is one example of a home mill, but there are many brands on the market. Some savvy home cooks even use a Vitamix to grind their own flours. Because of the design of most mills—stone grinding, without built-in screens—using a home mill automatically turns you into a whole-grain baker. The flavors are rich, and you avoid preservatives that industrial mills often use to make their flours last longer on shelves. Plus, when you choose whole-grain options for your home baking in this way, you're wasting less of each bushel of wheat grown, since so much of the good stuff won't get separated out at the milling stage (as with white bread).

 LOOK IT UP: You can geek out on grains, from breeding and baking to milling and fermenting, by attending Grain School, a three-day seminar hosted by the University of Colorado at Colorado Springs, or the Grain Gathering, a conference hosted by the Bread Lab at Washington State University.

10

ARSENIC AND RICE

A rsenic. The poisoner's weapon of choice. Around the world, the most common cause of arsenic poisoning is actually contaminated drinking water. The issue is particularly notorious in Bangladesh, for example. But here in the United States, it's rice that should be on your radar.

Remember the periodic table of elements from high school chemistry class? Arsenic is a natural element found in the mineral content of the earth's crust. It seeps into the air, water, and soil.

Arsenic is a serious toxin, according to almost every government agency that has a say on the matter. Some other crops absorb arsenic, but rice is an especially hazardous vehicle for it because of the way rice is grown, which is by flooding rice paddies. The roots of the rice crop absorb arsenic that gets released from the soil and store it in the grain. Rice contains anywhere from ten to twenty times as much arsenic as other cereal grains, according to a report from the British Broadcasting Corporation (BBC).

Rice is a staple around the world for many reasons, and most of us don't need to worry too much about the arsenic issue. Infants and young children are of greatest concern, though, because of the relative concentration they can consume in instant rice cereal, which can be dangerously high proportional to their body weight. The main health concerns of too much exposure are increased risk of heart disease; skin, bladder, and lung cancers; and compromised brain development and immune systems in children (from exposure as infants or in the womb). According to tests conducted by

Consumer Reports in 2015, "one serving of either [rice cereal or rice pasta] could put kids over the maximum amount of rice we recommend they should have in a week." For this reason, the advocacy branch of Consumer Reports has been fighting for a legal limit of arsenic in infant rice cereals since 2012. Parents are usually instructed to start babies on fortified rice cereal in order to provide iron in their babies' diets. The US Food and Drug Administration (FDA) has proposed but not adopted an official standard, so consumers are left waiting for rice cereals and other rice-based foods (such as rice milk) to have this protection put in place. Fortunately, other fortified infant cereals like barley and oatmeal are excellent sources of iron as well.

Although there may be other reasons to buy organic rice, arsenic content isn't one of them. The arsenic comes primarily from the ground and is absorbed by the rice plant the same way whether it's organically or conventionally grown. Where the rice is grown can make more of a difference, as can the type of rice. That 2015 report from Consumer Reports found that brown basmati rice grown in California, India, or Pakistan had a third less arsenic per serving than other sources of brown rice. The other major rice-growing states of the United States— Arkansas, Louisiana, Mississippi, Missouri, and Texas—may have residual arsenic-containing pesticides that were for decades sprayed on cotton grown in those areas. Good to know, but it's a tall order to check the place of origin on every Chinese take-out dish or rice-based grocery product you buy.

HOW YOU CAN MINIMIZE ARSENIC INTAKE

Rinse raw rice before you cook it. Cook using a ratio of at least 6 cups water to 1 cup rice, and drain the remaining water afterward. According to Consumer Reports, these three techniques can lower arsenic exposure compared with the modern way of cooking rice to absorb all the water in which it cooks.

MINIMIZE ARSENIC INTAKE BY RINSING RAW RICE, USING 6 CUPS
OF WATER TO COOK, AND DRAINING EXCESS WATER AFTER COOKING.

Eat a variety of grains, versus just lots of rice. I was especially bummed to learn that brown rice has about 80 percent more arsenic than white rice. It's because of the otherwise noble germ, which gets removed to produce white rice. Unfortunately, arsenic accumulates in that outer layer. This does *not* mean that eating white rice is your only option for avoiding arsenic. Loads of intact whole grains have nutritional profiles similar to that of brown rice and are just as delicious. They're similarly fluffy and nutty to use in a wide range of meals. They include:

amaranth // barley // buckwheat // bulgur // farro // millet // oatmeal // polenta or grits

Diversify. If you have a habit of ordering the same brown rice bowl from a restaurant or snacking on rice cakes every afternoon, mix it up. I have had this very snack habit myself, because of my profound fondness for a product from Lundberg Family Farms: dark-chocolate-covered brown rice cakes. Lundberg tests all its products for arsenic and publishes the results, which consistently fall under the draft FDA level for infant cereal and well under the level from the European Food Safety Authority for brown rice. But even if I had this habit with a brand that wasn't so committed to transparency, my arsenic discovery wouldn't mean I should ban brown rice cakes from my diet. It would mean I should diversify my snack routine.

11

SUGARS:
IN DEFENSE OF FRUIT

Milk and yogurt contain sugar. It's called lactose. Fruit contains sugar. It's called fructose. These are not to be treated with the same evil eye as added sugar. Why? The company they keep. When you eat these foods, you're consuming the naturally present sugars in a package with other beneficial components. And how you consume them—in what form, in what quantity, over what period of time—makes a big difference in how healthy they are.

Under the heading of "good intention, wrong abstention," you'll find people who avoid healthy foods that naturally contain sugar out of fear that these foods will do damage like added sugar does.

Sugar in fruit doesn't cause insulin to spike in the same way sugar in other forms does. It's all about keeping the cell walls intact. That's how you get the most out of fiber. The sugars effectively get sequestered in the fruit's cells, and it takes a long time for the digestive tract to break down those cells. The sugars therefore enter the bloodstream slowly, giving the liver more time to metabolize them. Four apples may contain the same amount of sugar as 24 ounces of soda, but the slow rate of absorption minimizes any surge in blood sugar. Repeated surges make the pancreas work harder and can contribute to insulin resistance, increasing the risk for type 2 diabetes.

Sugar eaten in fruit has not been tied to negative health outcomes. Instead, higher fruit intake has been linked to lower body weight and reduced risk of obesity-related illnesses.

WHOLE FRUIT FIRST

In terms of impact on blood sugar, this is the hierarchy of sugar sources you should aim for, i.e., the ideal places and forms from which to derive natural sweetness in your diet:

1 WHOLE FRUIT *(fresh or frozen)*

2 DRIED FRUIT *(just the fruit, no added sugar)*

3 SMOOTHIE *(aka fruit in liquid form, no added sugar)*, blended from whole fruit, with skins and pulp included

4 JUICE *(aka fruit in liquid form, no added sugar)*, ideally freshly squeezed

Why is that? Whole fruits contain healthful antioxidants and nutrients, for one. And because it takes longer to break down the fiber-rich scaffolding of fruit, it moves farther down our intestines and triggers the hormones that make us feel full, so we're less likely to eat too much at once. Fruit's fiber helps various kinds of healthy bacteria thrive, which can enhance our gut microbiome. (More on this in "Fermented Foods and Fiber" on page 53.) The amount of fiber varies by fruit type—from about 3 grams per medium-sized orange or banana to 8 grams per cup of raspberries, the highest of all. (You're aiming for a total of about 28 grams per day.) Be sure to eat the skins of fruits like apples and pears, since they hold much of the fiber.

Fruit in liquid form, on the other hand, acts like an instant sugar injection. It's very easy to drink a lot of juice in a short amount of time, and that much sugar is hard for your digestive system to handle. This is not to say that juice can't be part of most people's diets. It offers vitamins and minerals and sometimes fiber, and it can hydrate you if water isn't doing the trick or isn't available. But you're best off keeping your total consumption to a minimum. Opt for juices with nothing added and nothing subtracted.

Lastly, a word on dried fruit and how that fits into the picture. Its main drawback is the same as that of juice: It's easier than with whole fruit to consume too many calories in one sitting because the calories and sugar are concentrated into smaller, more efficient delivery packets, which makes for a worse metabolic impact. But because that key cellular structure remains intact, it's still better than juice. And depending on what's available to you, if it's a choice between eating dried fruit or no fruit at all, dried fruit is definitely worth it, given its long shelf life, low price, and portability.

12

FAT IN FOOD: THE ESSENTIALS

You may have heard people say that we don't have to worry about fat anymore, and to that I say, well, no and yes. No, we don't have to worry about how much fat, but yes, we do need to worry about what kind.

There are four main types of fat: trans, saturated, monounsaturated, and polyunsaturated.

Trans fat: Avoid altogether. Though this type of fat can be found in meat and milk, the majority consumed in the US is the artificial kind. It's mostly solid at room temperature, and high levels of it are found in margarine, shortening, and processed foods with "partially hydrogenated oils" as an ingredient. By 2020, the year this book is published, they should be phased out of the food supply. No longer "Generally Recognized as Safe" by the FDA, trans fat is bad news all around. It raises "bad" cholesterol (LDL) and promotes blood clot formation, which can lead to heart attacks and strokes. Trans fat is also tied to insulin resistance (a precursor to diabetes) and a host of other health issues.

Saturated fat: Keep to a minimum. Solid at room temperature, saturated fat is found at high levels in butter, dairy, and red meat (usually beef, pork, and lamb). It raises bad cholesterol (LDL) *and* "good" cholesterol (HDL), but high intake overall is associated with higher risk of heart disease. Heed the daily limit of about 13 grams as recommended by the American Heart Association—that's the amount found in a little over two glasses of whole milk, a little under 2 tablespoons of butter, *or* 1 heaping tablespoon of coconut oil.

Oils that are liquid at room temperature are a sign of relatively low saturated fat content. Think vegetable oil versus butter. Or how "oils" like palm and coconut are actually semisolid at room temperature; that's a clear tip-off of saturated fat content.

Monounsaturated fat: Make it the majority of your total fat intake, along with polyunsaturated fat. It's liquid at room temperature, and sources with high levels of it include olive oil, canola oil, and peanut oil, as well as avocados and nuts. It lowers LDL and can raise HDL in certain cases.

Polyunsaturated fat: With essentially the same health effects as monos, and also liquid at room temperature, polyunsaturated fat sources include whole grains, fish like sardines and salmon, and seeds like sunflower and safflower. Polyunsaturated fat gets special points for omega-3s, which have other health-promoting properties like keeping heart rates steady. This

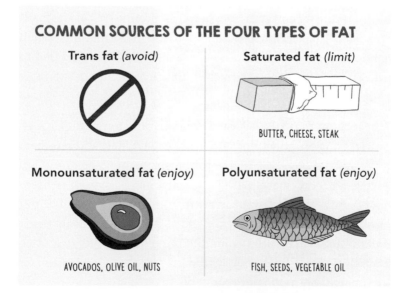

COMMON SOURCES OF THE FOUR TYPES OF FAT

Trans fat (avoid)

Saturated fat (limit)

BUTTER, CHEESE, STEAK

Monounsaturated fat (enjoy)

AVOCADOS, OLIVE OIL, NUTS

Polyunsaturated fat (enjoy)

FISH, SEEDS, VEGETABLE OIL

is useful in preventing death from heart disease and offers benefits to the immune system and brain function, not to mention eyesight and conditions like eczema. Aim for at least one serving of foods rich in omega-3s per day. (If you're pregnant or trying to become pregnant, this is especially important.) High sources of omega-3s include not only the foods mentioned above but walnuts, dark green leafy vegetables, and flaxseeds. In the animal kingdom, turn to fish, the fattier the better: not only salmon and sardines, but tuna, mackerel, and herring. And although you can get omega-3s from grass-fed beef, it's not the best source. Omega-6s are something some people are concerned about, too, but getting them takes less proactive measures than consuming omega-3s.

All fats—animal or plant—contain combinations of saturated and unsaturated fatty acids. It's inevitable to get some of the not-so-good saturated fats carried along with your good monos and polys. When you consume appropriate, healthy amounts of fats, the good monos and polys outweigh the saturated.

SIX SIMPLE SWAPS TO REPLACE SATURATED FATS WITH UNSATURATED FATS:

1 Sauté vegetables with vegetable oil, rather than butter.

2 Rather than spreading bread with butter, dip it in olive oil.

3 Bake cookies with canola oil, rather than shortening.

4 Cook fish or chicken for dinner, rather than beef or pork.

5 Enjoy nuts and seeds as snacks, rather than a pastry or cookie.

6 Check the ingredients list and choose foods with canola or soybean oil over palm or coconut oil.

13

FROM SOY TO NUTS, PLANT-BASED "MILKS"

Plant-based milks have blossomed on grocery-store shelves in recent years—from almond to soy, oat to flax—and that's good news, because regular dairy milk isn't the be-all and end-all. So, if you're already there with an "alt milk" (as about 40 percent of a nationally representative sample of Americans who buy milk products are), or you're thinking about getting on board, here's what you need to know.

HEALTH

Nutritionally, plant-based milks vary by product, and though not a complete match with dairy milk's nutritional profile, for the most part, plant-based milks are on par. Traditionally, cow's milk has been the teacher's pet of the nutrition community: It's got lots of calcium, vitamin D, folate, and other vitamins and minerals, plus a good amount of protein. But most Americans get more than enough protein by eating a variety of foods throughout the day (granted, they're getting that protein from mostly animal products), so milk needn't be viewed as *the* source. Plus, cow's milk and cheese are high in saturated fat and calories (facts that, as a full-blown cheeseaholic, I hate to admit). Often they come from dairy cows pumped with hormones like estrogen and insulin-like growth factor, which have been linked to risks of several types of cancer. There are plenty of other ways to get your calcium needs.

For your health, soy, almond, and hemp milks are largely considered the best of the popular plant-based choices, and oat

THE HEALTH RUNDOWN ON POPULAR PLANT-BASED MILKS

SOLID CHOICES

Almond milk: Offers healthy fats and some key vitamins, including calcium in spades; lower in calories than cow's or soy milk.

Cashew milk, hazelnut milk, macadamia nut milk, peanut milk, walnut milk, and other nut milks: Usually comparable choices to almond milk as far as low calories and high nutritional value, though some are less widely available and/or more expensive.

Flax milk: Low in calories, high in those healthy, hard-to-get omega-3s.

Hemp milk: Offers healthy fats with omega-3s and a modest number of calories. Opt for the kind fortified with calcium and vitamins D and B12.

Oat milk: Nutrients are solid, including a high fiber score, and calories are comparable to cow's milk.

Soy milk: High marks for overall nutrition, but if you're low on vitamins D and B12, get soy milk fortified with those nutrients, or look to other sources like eggs and those small fatty fish like sardines.

NOT AS GREAT

Coconut milk: Can be lower in calories but has a higher proportion of saturated fat.

Rice milk: Relatively high in calories, given that it doesn't offer much as far as nutrients.

milk is another good option. Flax milk is my personal favorite. Soy has stirred much controversy, particularly around breast cancer risk, though the research is inconclusive so far. Soy foods appear to be healthy for most people, but until more research is conducted, it's best to consume them in moderation versus multiple times a day. And for all milks, plant or otherwise, be sure to opt for unsweetened versions. As with chocolate milk, sometimes the flavored ones pack sugars well beyond what's found naturally in the core ingredient. Skipping milk altogether can be a simple way to trim a few calories if you're watching those. Many Americans are low on potassium and vitamin D, two nutrients that cow's milk offers (through fortification for the latter), so if this is a concern and you switch to a plant milk, check the labels for comparable levels, or rely on other, higher sources of these nutrients—such as sweet potatoes, spinach, and bananas for potassium, and mushrooms or fatty fish like herring and sardines for vitamin D.

LACTOSE INTOLERANCE

Twenty-five to 40 percent of adults globally cannot digest the sugar in cow's milk. Among the tens of millions of Americans estimated to be lactose intolerant are up to 80 percent of African Americans, Ashkenazi Jews, and Latinx, 95 percent of Asian Americans, and 80 to 100 percent of Native Americans. That's according to a report from the National Institutes of Health. It's really just those of northern European descent who have an easy time with milk. This means that when you get right down to it, the existing government recommendation on milk is awfully inconsiderate. And in fact, people of color are far more likely than white people to buy nondairy milk.

PLANET

Plant-based milks are an upgrade in planet protection. Anything involving cows requires a ton of water because of all the feed you have to grow. A stunning 98 percent of milk's water footprint stems from the cow's diet, much of which is alfalfa, a super water-intensive crop. The rest comes from cows being greedy guzzlers, requiring 23 gallons of water per day per cow, compared with our human hydration requirement of 1 gallon per day per person.

So, as you think about your morning coffee and which milk to buy (if at all), consider that, all told, producing a 1-gallon jug of regular milk takes about 2,000 gallons of water. Almond and soy milks require roughly one-sixth and one-half that amount, respectively (though exact numbers vary).

GENERALLY SPEAKING, ALMOND, SOY, AND OTHER PLANT-BASED
MILKS REQUIRE MUCH LESS WATER THAN COW'S MILK.

STICKING WITH COW'S MILK? HERE ARE SIGNALS OF HIGHER ANIMAL WELFARE STANDARDS

The typical treatment standards for dairy cows in this country are not so hot. Dairy cows' natural behavior is to graze on pasture, yet 80 percent are raised only indoors, without access to such fields. You can pick better cow's milk products by checking for these attributes and labels on the carton:

Pasture-raised. Because a cow is not confined in close quarters with other animals, this label means the animal is less likely to get sick and need antibiotics—plus it confers some health benefits because of healthy fats in the grasses. Third-party certifications assuring pasture-raised include "American Grassfed" and "PCO Certified 100% Grassfed" (the latter from the USDA-accredited certifying agency Pennsylvania Certified Organic).

No growth hormones were used. Unfortunately, "no rBGH" or "no rBST" (recombinant bovine growth hormone or recombinant bovine somatotropin, the two names for the hormone most commonly given to cows to stimulate milk production) aren't verified claims. So, for assurance of no growth hormones, look for "USDA Organic," "Certified Humane Raised and Handled," "Animal Welfare Approved," "American Humane Certified," and "American Grassfed." Widely available in supermarkets, they sometimes cost more.

Not fed animal by-products. Dairy cows are natural herbivores, so they should be eating only vegetarian feed. Unfortunately, the FDA has for decades allowed producers to cut corners by feeding leftover animal parts from slaughterhouses as well as animal poop to food-producing animals like cows and chickens. "Vegetarian-fed" on its own is not regulated, though, so for assurance of species-appropriate feed, look for most of the same labels as those indicating pasture-raised or no growth hormones used, along with a few others found at *greenerchoices.org*.

14

FERMENTED FOODS AND FIBER

When we eat food, it travels down our intestinal tract, known less elegantly as our "gut." Along the journey, it encounters trillions of bacteria. But these bacteria come in peace. Collectively, they make up the gut microbiome. This is the center of a newish category of medicine that has uncovered ties between an unhealthy gut and a host of ailments—from colon cancer to diabetes, allergies to asthma.

"These microbes are like factory workers keeping the body's operations running smoothly, playing essential roles in digestion, revving up the immune system, protecting us from pathogens, and regulating metabolism." So explains a great guide to microbes published in *Cooking Light* magazine. They also tap specialized cells—neurons—to communicate nerve signals via the "gut-brain axis," as it's called, and help maintain steady blood sugar levels.

So far, research suggests that those of us living in Western countries have alarmingly lower levels of microbial diversity compared with what would be optimal for health. Theories abound about why, but it may have to do with our limited exposure to nonthreatening germs in our environments: overly sanitized indoor spaces versus playing outside or working on farms, as more people used to do, and excessive intake of ultra-processed foods and antibiotic use. Even cesarean sections and feeding babies formula versus breast milk have been implicated, as exposure seems especially important early in life.

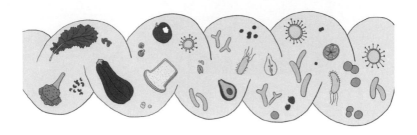

To correct this, all signs point to fiber as the ticket to a thriving community of gut bacteria. Although fiber is dubbed a "nutrient of public health concern," only about 5 percent of American adults and children eat the recommended amount of about 28 grams a day (though the exact target depends on one's sex and age). On average, we consume roughly half that recommended amount.

Found in fruits, vegetables, whole grains, nuts, beans, and seeds, the plant fibers we're talking about are the key food source for bacteria. Just like when you have a pet, you can't forget to feed it. And with 68 percent of Americans owning a pet, I think that's an idea we can pretty much all get on board with. These types of fiber are called *prebiotics*. Because they help microbes grow, prebiotics have been likened to fertilizers for your gut. From berries to bananas, bulgur to broad beans, fiber is fantastic. It helps create a strong immune system and boosts metabolism.

So, eat foods with fiber while also aiming to ensure sufficient sources of naturally occurring *probiotics* in your diet. Probiotics are not food for bacteria but actual strains of bacteria—living organisms—that you add to the current residents in your gut when you eat foods that contain them. From yogurt to kefir, kimchi to sauerkraut, and kombucha galore, probiotics are most often found in foods that have been fermented. You might recognize the fine-print "live and active cultures" from a yogurt container, along with ingredients like *Lactobacillus bulgaricus* or *Streptococcus thermophilus*.

NOW IT'S TIME FOR SOME CRITICAL CAVEATS:

* First, the research on the microbiome is still in its early days. Although it's incredibly promising, there's much we don't yet know, such as how eating a certain diet affects the immune system, in terms of general human biology, and about unique differences between people based on various health conditions like allergies—the personalized dimension of the diet-microbiome connection.

* Some fiber is better than others. Dozens of additives are used in mostly junk food products so the manufacturers can list high fiber attributes on the package. These "isolated fibers" are distinguished from fiber occurring naturally in foods. You're better off with the fiber found in real, whole foods (the beneficial package of an apple, say).

* Dietary supplements, whether they're prebiotics, probiotics, or some other nutrient, aren't well regulated. In general, you should treat them with more wariness than whole foods. Plus, one pill doesn't seem to have nearly the same effect for fostering a *diverse* microbial community, which is as important as its total population. Check with your doctor before taking a supplement of any kind.

 LOOK IT UP: If all this really revs your engine, check out *uBiome.com* and have your stool analyzed. The test results will provide your gut's unique microbial portrait.

15

POLLINATOR PROTECTION

Many of us love honey in our tea and on our Cheerios, in our salad dressing and on our Greek yogurt. But have you ever wondered how it gets to us in that cute little bear bottle? It's from bees regurgitating nectar they collect from flowering plants. Bee stomachs (technical term: *crops*) act as storage units. The forager bee who harvests the nectar deposits the honey into the stomach of a processor bee, who posts up at the entrance of the hive, delivering the nectar himself or herself into the honeycomb.

Honey and honeybees relate to your plate for reasons far above their enterprising spirit. All living organisms aim to leave behind a future generation, but most plants can produce offspring (seeds) only when pollen gets transferred from the male of one of their flowers to a female. This can happen via the wind, but also via insects, butterflies, birds, bees, and other pollinators. Some 90 percent of wild plants and 30 percent of the world's crops—the apples and the blueberries, the almonds and the pumpkins—can't live or produce food without cross-pollination. When a bee pays a flower a visit, the pollen gets stuck to/shaken off the bee's body while it's stationed there, sucking out nectar. Although bees aren't the only pollinators we've got, they're one of the most important.

Bees are running out of nectar. Wild bee populations have been collapsing in large part because of climate change. With warmer temperatures, many flowers bloom before or after the time bees are used to, so by the time they arrive, the flower has come and gone or not yet arrived, so there's no pollen or nectar to be had. Loss of wild habitat—in household gardens, on farms, in once-wild places cleared for development—also leaves fewer plants for pollinators to visit. And, no surprise, a particular class of pesticides, neonicotinoids, meant to kill pests, also harms honeybees. These chemicals are widely used not only on farms but in home gardens.

This is concerning because all together, pollinators—and especially bees—support more than 250,000 species of plants that not just we humans but animals depend on for our food supply. Of all those pollination-dependent crops, 80 percent rely on bees specifically.

WHAT CAN YOU DO TO HELP?

* Buy food that's grown without those pesticides. You can also choose foods grown by farmers engaged in habitat preservation and planting pollinator-friendly flowers interspersed among their crops. Ask about them at your farmers' market.

* To be a conscious eater, in this case, be a conscious gardener. Avoid neonics yourself by choosing live garden plants grown without them. Thankfully, big home and garden retailers like Home Depot and Lowe's have committed to phasing out neonics over time, and those still treated with them will usually be labeled as such. You can also help by not using the pesticide yourself on the plants you grow. Consult the website of the Xerces Society for Invertebrate Conservation (*xerces.org*) for the common

types of neonicotinoids—which are scientific-looking, multisyllabic words like imidacloprid—and names of home garden products that use them, like BioAdvanced 3-in-1 Insect, Disease & Mite Control. Instead, practice what's called integrated pest management. Plant flowers to make up a healthy pollinator habitat: Best practices include planting a variety of flower colors and shapes, opting for native plants, and selecting flowers that bloom at different times of year to provide more months of nectar and pollen. Local nurseries can help guide you.

* Whether you garden or not, provide nesting sites for pollinators, from hummingbirds and butterflies to bats and bees. The US Fish and Wildlife Service website (*fws.gov*) has tips.

16

A GENTLE RAIN ON
THE PLANT-BASED PARADE

About 39 percent of Americans are trying to eat more plant-based foods. That's according to a 2018 Nielsen survey and is rather impressive, I must say. A diet that is entirely plant based, also known as *vegan*, is made up of fruits, vegetables, grains, nuts, legumes, plant-based oils, herbs, spices, water, beer, and wine—you get the picture. Not allowed is anything involving animals in any way in the making of the food. The list is long, but most obviously, this means no cheese, milk, butter, meat, or fish. Depending on one's philosophy as a vegan, it might also include honey. (By comparison, vegetarian means not eating animals directly, so no meat or fish, but ingredients derived from animals, like milk and cheese, are fine.) But the plant-based movement, like many social movements, has gotten a little ahead of its skis in one crucial respect: nutrition.

Although better than animal-based foods as far as respecting the environment, animals themselves, and various cultural and religious sensitivities, plant-based foods are not *automatically* healthier. Being a conscious eater relies on a nuanced assessment of what you're putting in your body. Beware magic bullet mentality and treat plant-based substitutes—the milks, the cheeses, the burger patties, the yogurts, the cold cuts, the coconut macaroons—with subtle skepticism. It's absolutely possible to eat a vegan diet that is as healthy as or even healthier than an omnivorous diet. But it's equally possible to eat a really crummy vegan diet. Look out for these things before jumping aboard the plant-based bandwagon:

Just because a food is vegan does not mean it is healthy. French fries can be vegan. Doughnuts can be vegan. I'm a little fuzzy on what exactly Gatorade is made of, but I'm pretty sure it's vegan. Knowing an item is vegan is not license to eat vegan junk food in spades—at least for those who still want to feel good about their responsible food choices. Heaps of press have been poured upon the Impossible Burger, for example, a remarkably beef-like vegan burger that "bleeds." It's made primarily of soy protein concentrate, coconut oil, sunflower oil, and "natural flavors." From personal experience, I agree with the masses: It tastes just as juicy and satisfying as a regular burger. But the original Impossible Burger, which people ate for years, packed 70 *percent* of the Daily Value for saturated fat and 25 percent of the Daily Value for sodium—more than two times as much saturated fat and seven times as much sodium as a lean beef burger. The 2019 version was an improvement but still loads on nearly half the Daily Value for saturated fat.

Many plant-based substitutes are highly processed. The ingredient lists for many vegan alternatives are not necessarily short or full of words you can pronounce. The ingredient profile of a frozen vegan sausage patty, for example, is no angel. Often to mimic the taste and texture of animal-based counterparts, manufacturers rely on all kinds of technologies and additives. So, if you're going plant-based, think twice before loading up on soy protein isolate and heme, since there's a lot we don't know yet about their long-term health effects. I prefer to enjoy vegan dishes featuring whole foods like legumes, produce, nuts, and whole grains from cuisines around the world where these foods have been central for centuries. They know a thing or two about making the flavor of those ingredients really pop.

Can you maintain it? As with most diets, eating only plant-based foods can, for many people, feel restrictive. For this reason, my colleagues at The Culinary Institute of America and the Harvard T. H. Chan School of Public Health suggest that Americans aim for "plant-forward" diets. As part of an initiative I lead called Menus of Change®, plant-forward eating and cooking "emphasizes and celebrates, but is not limited to, plant-based foods." It's all about readjusting the ratios of plant and animal foods compared with typical American diets. Though it can include vegan and vegetarian ways of eating, it's a bigger-tent approach. Michael Pollan's famed words—"Eat food. Not too much. Mostly plants"—include that key modifier: *mostly*. Near synonyms for this way of eating are *flexitarian* and *plant-rich*. If you're committed to going all the way, props to you; thanks to the many fabulous, truly healthy vegan options now available through restaurant menus, meal kits, and grocery store shelves, not to mention inspiring vegan blogs, it's *way* easier to be a vegan for life than it once was. But for the 97 percent of us who don't see that happening, keep in mind that both nutritionally and environmentally, you still cover a lot of ground by simply improving the ratios of what you eat over time. Some folks find success with routines like Mark Bittman's VB6—eating only vegan options before 6 p.m.—or Meatless Monday or Green Monday; others find they can eat mostly plant-based during the week and save meat to enjoy as a weekend treat. Make the effort, make the adjustment, and make it work for you, your lifestyle, and your family for the long term.

17

HOW TO CHOOSE A COOKING OIL

Walk into any grocery store and you'll often find the number of cooking oils overwhelming. Walnut and peanut, soy and corn, avocado and grapeseed . . . whatever "vegetable" is in "vegetable oil" (usually soybeans, it turns out). On top of all the flavors, who's got a clue what an "expeller" is, or why you'd want your oil to be pressed in one? How, I wonder, does a virgin become *extra* virgin?

The bottom line is this: For health, versatility, and production methods, olive oil is a great go-to for pretty much all your daily cooking. Canola is a stellar backup act.

Taste and cost: The importance of these factors will likely vary based on how often you're using an oil and what those uses are. Specialty oils like walnut and flaxseed might be superb nutritionally, but they are tough to sustain financially if you're using them every day. Ditto for toasted sesame oil, whose smoky richness is welcome at times but doesn't jibe with every dish. So, you'll want a default cooking fat you can use on a regular basis, both for taste and for cost.

Nutrition profile: Focus on the type of fat, not the total. In practice, this means choosing plant oils over animal fats. What's best for your health happens to also be best for the planet.

Smoke point: Different fats and oils break down at different high temperatures, releasing smoke and a bad smell into the air. When that happens, no one within shouting range is a happy camper. The rule of thumb on smoke points is that the more refined an oil is, the higher its smoke point. Refining means extracting the liquid from the nut, seed, or fruit by using heat and a chemical solvent. This makes the oil lighter in color, gives it a longer shelf life, and results in a more neutral flavor, in large part because it removes a lot of the antioxidants. Expeller pressing involves only a mechanical press, no solvent. Cold pressing is similar to expeller pressing except it occurs under cooler temperatures, which can preserve flavor and antioxidants.

Exact numbers vary by producer and how long an oil has been sitting on your shelf, but generally speaking, here are some common cooking oils' smoke points.

HIGH SMOKE POINTS
(good for deep-frying, stir-frying, searing, and grilling)

Refined (aka "regular" or "light") olive oil	465°F
Peanut oil	450°F
Sunflower oil	440°F

MEDIUM SMOKE POINTS
(good for sautéing, moderate-temp roasting, and baking)

Canola oil	400°F
Regular (untoasted) sesame oil	350°F–410°F
Extra-virgin olive oil	325°F–375°F

LOW SMOKE POINTS
(good for finishing a dish with a drizzle or for dressing)

Extra-virgin olive oil	325°F–375°F
Walnut oil	320°F
Flaxseed oil	225°F

Production methods and point of origin: Production practices vary widely for different cooking fats. There's the land to grow or raise the original thing (such as olives or dairy cows). There are the farming practices used to grow or raise that thing (for example, organic or not, grass-fed or not). And there are the processing practices used to turn that thing into a finished product.

Purely in terms of carbon and water footprints, sunflower and canola rank the best. Thanks to all the cows involved, butter's carbon and water footprints are far worse than those of vegetable oils.

Palm oil is an environmental nightmare. The trees are grown in tropical locations, and the oil production threatens endangered species like orangutans and Sumatran tigers; pollutes the air through burning to clear forests to make room for palm plantations; pollutes freshwater, affecting people relying on that water downstream; and contributes to soil erosion and climate change because of the destruction of carbon-storing trees. More than half of packaged products purchased in the United States, from cookies to lipstick to detergent, include palm oil. Though used less often in American cooking, it's the most commonly consumed plant oil in the world. Some food products tout sustainably produced palm oil, but because palm oil is not even in the running for top oils nutritionally—it's about 50 percent saturated fat, whereas all the other plant oils are well under 20 percent—why bother?

With both soy and corn oils, the main concerns are about monoculture on a massive scale, which degrades soil health and usually involves lots of pesticides. Little information is available about canola production, but the main concern is that almost all of it is genetically engineered; if you're worried about that, opt for organic. Olive oil doesn't get off altogether, as its long-sustainable production practices haven't been entirely maintained as demand has skyrocketed beyond the original Mediterranean region. But by and large, the trees are hardy, requiring little water, and as opposed to behemoth industrial farms, olive oil production is mostly done by small-scale family growers.

For processing techniques, refined oils are of concern because a solvent called hexane is typically used in the extraction process. Considered a neurotoxin by the CDC, it poses health concerns for factory workers who inhale it in high levels, from dizziness in the short term to blurred vision and numbness in the long term. Hexane also pollutes the air. So, no thanks. This issue presents a consumer conundrum, because refined oils tend to cost less. They also handle high temps better, so they don't release toxic compounds in your kitchen. Sounds like you can't win, right? This is where we get radically practical:

1   Those refined oils are best used when cooking at really high temperatures—but since fried foods are doing you no favors health-wise and grilled foods have risks we'll explore later in the book, the environmental impact of the oils is another reason to use them on occasion, versus every day.

2   Buy extra-virgin oil if you can afford it. Extra-virgin is an unrefined oil held to strict standards of quality, acidity, taste, and nutrient content. It means no hexane was used, nor was the crop treated with any chemicals or heat to remove the oil. Expeller-pressed or cold-pressed versions also mean no hexane and that only mechanical pressure was used.

3   Ditto for USDA-certified organic oils. Thanks to economies of scale, organic versions of more ubiquitous oils like olive and canola are relatively affordable, versus more obscure specialty oils like avocado and hazelnut.

18

THE OLIVE OIL VS. COCONUT OIL SHOWDOWN

A rguably the two most top-of-mind cooking oils are olive and coconut. Here's the gist of why olive is the winner.

WHY OLIVE OIL?

Thanks to plenty of scientific research, we know that olive oil has protective effects against a vast array of diseases and even the overall risk of premature death. It has among the highest percentages of monounsaturated fats of any cooking fat, along with antioxidants in the extra-virgin oil. Olive oil has a high enough smoke point to be useful in everyday cooking and baking and is low on the list of cooking fats carrying social or environmental baggage.

WHY NOT COCONUT OIL?

Compared with a tablespoon of olive oil, a tablespoon of coconut oil contains about six times the amount of saturated fat. Although some research has linked the main type of saturated fatty acid in coconut oil, lauric acid, to increased levels of HDL, or "good" cholesterol, it still appears to raise LDL, or "bad" cholesterol.

Proponents of coconut oil point out that it is rich in phytochemicals that have healthful antioxidant properties. Although it's true that extra-virgin coconut oil, like extra-virgin olive oil, contains phytochemicals, most of the coconut oil on the market is refined and provides few of those antioxidants. Even so, the high sat-fat content would far outweigh any benefit of the antioxidants.

And coconut oil is in hot water with Fair Trade USA because of the extreme poverty that coconut farmers endure in places like the Philippines. These are the growers behind not just coconut oil but coconut water and milk and cosmetic products.

Although coconut oil certainly isn't the magic bullet some claim, there's no need to avoid it completely, especially if you're using it in place of butter or shortening in baked goods, or to impart flavor in something like a curry dish or roasted sweet potatoes; there's a reason coconut oil plays a role in many cuisines around the world. As a general rule, though, if you're between the two, olive oil wins across the board.

SELECTING & STORING OLIVE OIL

1 **CHECK FOR A HARVEST DATE.** You want it as fresh as possible since the oil has been pressed from the fruit of olives; over time its healthy polyphenols (plant compounds) degrade, and it will go rancid. Though a harvest date is not nearly as common as the "best by" date, no more than 18 months from harvest is a better indicator of freshness.

2 **BUY SMALLER BOTTLES FOR DIRECT-FROM-BOTTLE USES.** That way you can enjoy the pungency of drizzled extra-virgin oil while it's fresh, ideally within six weeks of purchase.

3 **KEEP OLIVE OIL (AND PRETTY MUCH ALL YOUR VEGETABLE OILS) AWAY FROM *LIGHT, HEAT & AIR*.** They kill the oil's antioxidants, quashing many of the health benefits and the delicious flavor and aroma. Store your olive oil in a dark, cool place, like the back of your pantry, and definitely not in the cabinet above your stove. The best containers are a tin can, stainless steel, and dark glass, because they keep out the three enemies of quality. Clear glass with a wraparound label does a decent job as well. Colored plastic is better than clear, but it still isn't a good option because it is porous, letting in oxygen.

19

FREEZING
AND (GLOBAL) WARMING

A strawberry right off the vine. A cucumber with a satisfying crunch. A tomato still warm from the sun. A wild salmon eaten the day it was caught. You can see why *fresh* is among the most beloved adjectives in the American food lexicon.

But nutritionally speaking, frozen food is a revelation. (Caveat patrol: Plenty of products found in the frozen food aisles—from corn dogs to ice cream sandwiches—are only vaguely reminiscent of real food. They're highly processed, with nutrition profiles you don't want to shack up with.) Frozen food is also a winner for cutting down on food waste. And ditto for your grocery budget. Those fresh strawberries in the produce section may be delicious, but freezing them actually locks in nutrients, which gradually degrade as produce ripens over the course of transportation and while sitting out in grocery stores for your perusal or on your kitchen countertop for easy snacking. Plus—and of course it depends on the season—fresh can cost more than twice the price of frozen. Not to mention, it's not very responsible (or tasty!) to eat some types of fresh produce, like strawberries, year-round, since they're in peak season in most places only from about April through June.

Refrigeration is considered one of the greatest breakthroughs of the past two centuries. It has brought food safety, longer shelf life, less waste, higher nutrition, and, by moving fresh foods to places that need them through refrigerated trucks or railcar, access to food for those who don't live near fresh sources of it. We should be thankful to live in a time when we can cool our food (and our bodies) through the technology of refrigerants.

But here's the rub. Ironically, cooling actually leads to warming—global warming, that is. Number one on Project Drawdown's list of the most effective ways to reverse global warming is actually "refrigerant management." Sexy, huh? But it's serious business. What happens is that the chemicals that chill, both in refrigerators and in air conditioners, warm the atmosphere. Not because of how much greenhouse gases they emit (it's a fairly low level) but because of the way they trap heat. HFCs, which is short for hydrofluorocarbons, have anywhere from 1,000 to 9,000 times the warming effect that carbon dioxide does. Nearly 200 countries worldwide have already agreed to start phasing them out, but the issue is carefully handling the destructive refrigerants already in circulation. What does this mean to you as a consumer?

Enjoy your frozen foods conscientiously. Check the temperatures on your fridge and freezer. If they're lower than necessary, you're using a lot of excess energy. According to the US Department of Energy, aim for 35°F–38°F for the fridge part, and 0°F for the freezer. And ask yourself whether you really need that extra refrigerator in the garage. If you've got an old one (going on fifteen or twenty years), replacing it is a good

TO AVOID USING EXCESS ENERGY, AIM FOR 35°F TO 38°F FOR YOUR FRIDGE, AND 0°F FOR THE FREEZER.

idea not only because it's likely nowhere near as energy-efficient as it ought to be and is probably jacking up your energy bill, but because it was probably not manufactured with ozone-friendly refrigerants and insulation, which became the norm in 1995 and 2005 respectively. The EPA website, as well as Consumer Reports, can help.

Make sure your refrigerator doesn't have a leak. That's when the HFCs get released. (Same goes for your air-conditioning unit, if you have one.)

If you get a new refrigerator, make sure the old one gets disposed of properly. The EPA website (*epa.gov/rad/consumers*) has a handy guide on the steps to take.

20

SOS: SAVE OUR ~~SOULS~~ SOILS

Anyone who has read *The Grapes of Wrath* may have in mind clear images of the ominous black cloud that came roaring across the Plains states of this country in the 1930s. A massive environmental disaster created what is known as the Dust Bowl, but *dust* doesn't quite do justice to the magical material that was being disrupted. *Soil* is one of the most precious resources on planet Earth. Plant life, animal life, and the biodiversity of both all rely on the stuff. As does our entire food and water supply. Soil is also alive. Like our gut microbiomes, soils have their own microbiomes.

Although soil health is not yet a top-of-mind factor in most Americans' food decisions, there's a hint in the air from a growing movement of farmers, manufacturers, investors, and consumers that it soon will be. You may have already noticed that the growing practices showing up on food labels are expanding beyond just conventional versus organic. You may have seen biodynamic wines, for instance. And coming to a supermarket near you: regenerative agriculture.

You can think of it as organic *plus*. Or, put another way, rather than just doing less bad, regenerative agriculture does more good: The farming methods shift from simply not using stuff or doing stuff to the earth that's harmful to actively enriching the soil and the surrounding ecosystems—i.e., leaving the land even better than when you found it. Another way to think about the comparison is that organic agriculture is primarily about the process—*how* food is grown; regenerative agriculture is about the outcome or result—how the land, wildlife, water, and so forth *are affected by* the way food is grown.

There are ways to protect soil from eroding by using methods like cover crops and mulch. Less erosion means more carbon sequestered in the ground rather than released into the atmosphere. Carbon-capture methods are sorely needed if we as a planet have any chance at curbing total carbon emissions in time to avoid the worst effects of climate change. Adding compost and manure as a fertilizer instead of using synthetic fertilizers also builds soil organic matter, which means more nutrients that feed plants. This means more nutritious plants, healthier plants that require fewer pesticides, and even more flavorful plants.

Crop rotation is also key to both organic and regenerative practices, and it involves farmers planting a sequence of different crops on the same field each season. This too helps prevent soil erosion and builds that good organic matter to keep the soil healthy. It also disrupts insect infestation and plant diseases, increases biodiversity on the farm, and fixes nitrogen into the soil. This is in contrast to conventional monoculture practices—planting the same thing in abundance, most often corn and wheat and soy, year after year. A suite of damaging tactics, including annual tilling, are part of monoculture's package deal, releasing carbon that crops help store in the soil, which in turn has the aforementioned wrinkle of contributing to global warming.

What hurts the soil most often hurts the people who grow food on that soil. Years of intensive use of chemicals in California's San Joaquin Valley, for example, which produces much of the country's nuts and produce, have left cancerous contaminants in rural residents' drinking wells. These communities already suffer high rates of asthma and a devastating disease called valley fever, which comes from a toxic fungus in the soil. Accounting for the well-being of farmers may be regenerative agriculture's most novel feature. It recognizes

REGENERATIVE PRACTICES

Cover crops, compost, conservation tillage, crop rotation—all of these help store carbon, retain water, and build healthy soils.

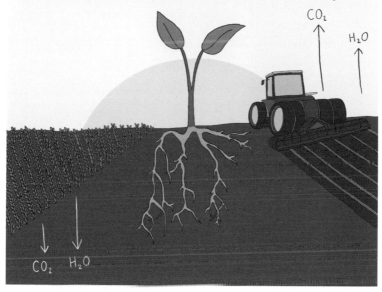

that without thriving farm communities, there is no farming. It strives for sustainability in the fullest sense, insisting that farmers can sustain their way of life and steward their land in ways that keep it fertile and productive for them, their families, and for all of us who rely on them to feed us.

CHOOSE FOODS THAT SUPPORT SOIL HEALTH

* Buy organic if you can afford it.

* Ask your farmers' market growers what soil-promoting practices they use (whether they're certified organic or not). Support those who use farm management practices like reduced or no-till (also called conservation tillage), cover crops, compost, and crop rotation, and who embrace

biodiversity—whether by growing multiple types of plants at once or by integrating plants and animals on the same farm, also called polyculture or diversified farming.

* At the grocery store, look for products with ingredients grown through regenerative agricultural practices. You can find those products by looking for a third-party label launched as a pilot in 2018 that's called "Regenerative Organic Certified." It includes the practices related to soil health described above, as well as others related to animal welfare and social justice. (*regenorganic.org*)

* In the near future, when dining out or selecting packaged foods, choose perennial crops when possible. Most crops get planted and tilled annually, which releases carbon into the atmosphere. Perennial crops (such as trees), by contrast, have deep roots. Kernza, a perennial grain, was the first prototype crop launched in the United States, sold for the first time commercially in Long Root Ale, a beer made by Patagonia Provisions. According to the Land Institute, in future years we'll see many more perennial products appear on shelves, like perennial sunflower oil and hummus from perennial legumes. Not eroding soil keeps carbon from being released (that's a good thing), but in addition, plants can actually pull existing carbon from the atmosphere (where it's damaging) and deposit it into the ground (where it's useful). This idea is called "carbon farming," meaning to pull carbon down from the sky, as opposed to only emitting it upward. The two efforts—not tilling/maintaining grasslands for prairie ecosystems, much like not deforesting/maintaining forests in rainforest ecosystems—work in concert. Choosing perennial crops isn't a magic bullet solution—just as with human health, there aren't any for environmental health—but it sure is a promising one.

21

STICKERS TO KNOW

What do all those little symbols and buzzwords mean on the side or bottom corner of a package? Beyond health, the third-party certification labels selected below are among the most meaningful signifiers of superior social or environmental considerations for stuff that comes from the ground. Some also appear on stuff that comes from animals as well as stuff you get from restaurant kitchens and factories. Some are regulated by federal agencies, and others are provided by advocacy groups or nongovernmental organizations (NGOs).

Align your values with these labels' assurances to decide where best to spend your extra grocery dollars.

CERTIFIED ORGANIC OR USDA ORGANIC

What it means: The standards prohibit a range of practices and substances, but it boils down to

* no synthetic pesticides,

* no growth hormones, and

* no antibiotics.

On a label for a processed food product, USDA organic certification means that 95 percent or more of the ingredients in the product were certified organic.

What it doesn't mean: That the product itself is nutritious. (Organic chocolate frosting is still chocolate frosting.) On animal-based foods, it also does not guarantee ambitious animal welfare standards, so if those are important to you, look for a label other than organic certification.

Who's behind it: US Department of Agriculture

Why it's legit: It has among the most rigorous and comprehensive standards as far as how a food is grown. In short, these standards can support ecosystems and farmworkers' health (though not necessarily their wages) because the farming practices are less intensive than conventional methods.

FAIRTRADE, FAIR FOR LIFE, AND FAIR TRADE CERTIFIED

What it means:
* good, safe working conditions on farms,
* prevents discrimination and harassment,
* prohibits forced labor and child labor, and
* a price premium is often fed into a fund for local projects.

Bananas are a common item I'd encourage you to buy fair trade certified.

What it doesn't mean: That workers are earning a *livable* wage. The three certifications ensure payment of minimum wage, but at the time you purchase a product, a manufacturer may only be gradually upping the pay of its workers. This means their livelihoods may not yet be as secure as you might imagine, depending on the cost of living in their area. For assurance of the highest pay, Consumer Reports considers Fair for Life to have the strongest policy of the three.

Who's behind it: Fairtrade International (with audits and inspections done by its certification body, FLOCERT); Europe-based ECOCERT; and Fair Trade USA, respectively

Why it's legit: In the words of Fairtrade International, "Not all trade is fair! Farmers and workers at the beginning of the chain don't always get a fair share of the benefits of trade. Fairtrade enables consumers to put this right." All of the standards described above involve rigorous inspections to verify compliance.

BIRD FRIENDLY

What it means: Used for coffee specifically, which is grown in the tropics, the sticker includes the organic standards but goes even further. It signals

* that the homes of migratory birds are respected,
* that insect biodiversity is maintained, and
* that coffee is grown in shade (the canopies of which can sequester carbon and help mitigate climate change).

These issues matter because forests typically get cut down as part of coffee production, and much wildlife habitat can be destroyed.

What it doesn't mean: That it applies to any products other than coffee. At least for now.

Who's behind it: The Smithsonian, specifically its National Zoo & Conservation Biology Institute

Why it's legit: Of all the coffee certification programs, this label is considered one of the most rigorous for habitat conservation.

BIODYNAMIC

What it means:

CERTIFIED
BIODYNAMIC

* Ensures that growers use methods that promote water conservation, soil health, and animal welfare while treating wetlands, grasslands, and forests as part of a self-sustaining farm as a whole.

* Rather than relying on fertilizers and fungicides, a grower draws solutions from within the farm as an ecosystem (such as animal manure).

* Requires that at least 10 percent of a farm's total land be off limits for farming in order to exist as a biodiversity preserve.

What it doesn't mean: That every product made from crops from that farm is biodynamic. Wine is the most common example. The grapes may have been biodynamically grown, but to be a biodynamic wine, the Demeter Processing Standards would also need to be met by the winemaker.

Who's behind it: Demeter USA, part of Demeter International

Why it's legit: With farms undergoing careful scrutiny through annual inspections, this label takes the organic standard as a baseline and pushes beyond merely not doing harm to the soil and surrounding ecosystems to actively helping them thrive.

TOP 5 TAKEAWAYS

1 What you already know is irrefutably true: Plants are the healthiest foods for humans.

2 Know the farming, know the food: For farmworkers' and critters' sake, pick organic, biodynamic, regenerative, and pollinator friendly.

3 Eat a variety of seasonal produce. It's good for the planet and good for your health.

4 Empower yourself and your family by keeping contaminants, added sugar, refined grains, and unhealthy fats at bay.

5 Make fiber your friend by eating plenty of whole grains, legumes, fruits, and veggies each day.

PART 2

STUFF THAT COMES FROM ANIMALS

road consensus applies among all countries except the United States (as of this printing) that we need to do everything possible to fight the tide of climate change. And protecting the planet is arguably the single most important reason to reduce meat consumption.

I am by no stretch a vegan myself, but frankly, the planet needs more people to eat more plant-based foods and fewer animal-based foods. Generally speaking, animal-based foods are less efficient uses of natural resources because you're growing animal feed and relying on these creatures to convert that feed into food that humans eat, rather than just growing food for humans to eat directly. By just about every metric used to evaluate the environmental impact of making food, the plant kingdom beats the animal kingdom by a long shot.

Some people use the term *flexitarian* for a diet that conscientiously reduces meat consumption. It is not a vegetarian or vegan diet. It's a mostly vegetarian diet that might occasionally include meat and fish. You can still enjoy a burger. It simply urges us all to make a continually conscious effort to shift to eating mainly plant-based foods. In the aggregate, this approach could cut total livestock emissions in half. It could also greatly lower our individual risk for developing a major chronic illness, avoiding millions and millions of premature deaths around the globe. So—it's a good idea.

But not all meat is equally implicated. Cutting back on red meat is the most important and effective. To back up: In this book, I consider "meat" to be flesh from land animals that we eat—basically red meat plus poultry (chicken, duck, turkey, etc.)—and "red meat" to be meat from mammals. Most commonly in our country, red meat means beef, pork, and lamb, but the category can include goat, horse, veal, and mutton. Poultry, fish, and seafood are of much lower concern for human

THE LIGHTER FOOTPRINT OF PLANT FOOD VS. ANIMAL FOOD

GREENHOUSE GAS EMISSIONS: 20 TIMES

THAT'S HOW MUCH HIGHER THE CARBON FOOTPRINT IS OF PROTEIN FROM BEEF COMPARED WITH PLANT-BASED PROTEIN SOURCES, SUCH AS BEANS AND LENTILS.

WATER: 31 TIMES

THAT'S HOW MUCH MORE WATER IS REQUIRED IF YOU EAT A HAMBURGER FOR LUNCH INSTEAD OF A SALAD.

LAND: 20 TIMES

THAT'S HOW MUCH MORE LAND IT TAKES TO MAKE THE SAME AMOUNT OF PROTEIN FROM BEEF COMPARED WITH PLANT-BASED PROTEIN SOURCES, SUCH AS BEANS AND LENTILS.

and environmental health, though issues still abound regarding animal welfare. For a better planet and better health, we should look for delicious, satisfying ways to cut our red meat intake. Experts recommend aiming for a little under 4 ounces at most per week, or about one hamburger per week or two servings of steak per month, and at most 7 ounces of poultry per week, or approximately one large chicken breast.

It bears repeating: If each of us Americans ate less red meat, we'd make a meaningful difference in reducing global warming. Stunningly, our current average beef intake is the equivalent of three hamburgers per week, so cutting that out of our diets would remove the equivalent greenhouse gas emissions of all the SUVs in the United States. That's the calculation offered by author Mark Bittman in his book *Food Matters*. Or, to put it another way, I'll paraphrase a great quote I heard once: "You're better off driving your Hummer to go get a salad than driving your Prius to a barbecue."

Dairy has a big impact, too. We're encouraged to keep dairy to 250 grams per day, which is about a cup of yogurt or roughly eight slices of cheese—and increase our consumption of plant proteins like nuts and legumes to more than 4 ounces per day, or about four handfuls of almonds per day. In terms of daily habits, this translates to, for instance, replacing your standard weekday lunch of a deli sandwich stacked with cold cuts to options like power bowls or wraps that might feature farro, avocado, chickpeas, and roasted veggies. For a full list of the target intakes that align optimal nutrition with environmental sustainability, visit *eatforum.org/eat-lancet-commission*.

22

FOOD FRAUD

Years ago, I learned the saying in Parma, Italy, that the farther away from the town you travel, the worse the Parmigiano-Reggiano tastes. The cheese is a storied delicacy first perfected in the 1200s. Over time, it has earned a global status, easily garnering twenty dollars a pound. Like Champagne from France, only the cheese produced in designated parts of Italy can be considered true Parmigiano-Reggiano, and it must be aged at least a year. Its similar-looking cousin, Parmesan, whose trophy case is a bit more sparse, is still by no means a cheap cheese in the United States. When you age the Parmesan wheels, they dry (hence the desirable grating texture and nutty taste), but that shrinks the yield and affects manufacturers' bottom lines.

So in 2012, it was disturbing and yet easy to understand when news hit of a major Pennsylvania-based cheese producer cutting its product labeled 100 percent real Parmesan with cellulose. That's an FDA approved additive, made from wood pulp, which is essentially what paper is made of. Sawdust, some call it. What's it doing on your pasta? For the pre-grated kind sold in those little plastic tubs, it reduces clumping. And it acts as a filler. (It's also a common ingredient in processed foods that have "added fiber.") The manufacturer, Castle Cheese, was investigated by the FDA, and it turned out that *none* of the cheese was actually Parmesan. It was a blend of imitation cheese and by-products of other cheeses like mozzarella and Swiss. The company filed for bankruptcy in 2014, and its president, who pleaded guilty to criminal charges, was given a large fine and potential jail time.

Some other Parmesan suppliers were found guilty of similar cellulose padding, as well as adulterating the premium product with cheaper cheeses like cheddar. As much as 20 percent of hard Italian cheese made in the United States may be mislabeled, as reported on *Bloomberg* in 2016.

Food fraud doesn't stop in the cheese aisle, sadly. Seafood fraud may be among the most alarming categories. Approximately one-third of the seafood in this country is mislabeled. That's according to tests conducted from 2010 to 2012 by the ocean conservation organization Oceana. Sometimes Atlantic cod, which is severely overfished, was sold as orange roughy; sometimes rockfish was disguised as snapper; sometimes escolar was masquerading as white tuna. Other than the egregious breach of trust, why is this a problem? One example would be if, by attempting to minimize mercury exposure, you bought halibut but, thanks to mislabeling, ended up eating tilefish, which is high in mercury. A big reason mislabeling happens in the first place is to pass off low-value fish for high-value ones, or to sell illegally caught fish. For other products, food safety issues could arise, such as products containing common allergens when a label says otherwise.

Seafood fraud puts the livelihoods of subsistence fishers at risk, because their legitimate catch gets undermined by the illegitimate, while also threatening the availability of fish and seafood for coastal communities around the world who need it for basic nutrition. Here in the United States, where food is abundant and available in greater variety, the big issue is, well, being played.

Other adulterated products in recent years include olive oil (cut with cheaper soy and sunflower oils); counterfeit manuka honey (an uber-expensive sweetener from New Zealand, popular among health fanatics); and a well-covered incident of horse meat being mixed into ground beef.

WAYS TO DEFEAT THE DECEIT

Buy whole foods. This is the number-one tip from Larry Olmsted, author of *Real Food, Fake Food*. "You can't be fooled buying a whole Maine lobster, but your lobster bisque might well have no lobster at all," he said in an email. "The less you can see and the more processed the food, the more room for adulteration." For example, avoid any additives in ground coffee by buying whole coffee beans, he said. Buy Parmesan whole and grate it yourself. Wheels of cheese don't use cellulose. (Or if you insist on grated, check the label to be sure there's no cellulose.) Opting for foods closer to their natural forms will almost certainly taste better and save you money while you're at it, since you're doing the "processing" (grinding the beans, grating the cheese) yourself.

Buy from retailers committed to authenticating their products. Blockchain technology, a kind of massive online ledger, is being used by more and more retailers and food companies—Walmart, Kroger, and Wegmans, and Dole, Nestlé, Unilever, and Tyson Foods, to name a few. It allows them to track and verify the point of origin and production methods used along the food supply chain. This technology can help improve food safety, too, because of the ability to more rapidly and precisely trace a food to its source. Blockchain or not, you may soon see scannable QR codes or apps that offer consumers a new level of traceability. In the meantime, ask grocers and producers directly or consult their websites to learn how, if at all, they are using these tools and others to ensure your food is real.

Get your fish from top-ranked grocers. Each year, Greenpeace releases a retailer scorecard, "Carting Away the Oceans," that rates sustainable seafood across standards for both wild and farm-raised products; the extent to which a retailer actively helps improve fisheries and bodies of water it sources from;

how well it matches Seafood Watch's recommendations for twenty-six commonly sold species; and, importantly, labeling and transparency, which includes how carefully sourcing data gets tracked and communicated to customers. In the 2018 report, Whole Foods Market, Hy-Vee, and ALDI took the top three spots out of twenty-two major American grocers. They were considered "leading," whereas the bottom of the barrel was occupied by Wakefern and Save Mart (both considered "failing") and Price Chopper (which got a "passing" grade, though it just squeaked through by a few tenths of a percent).

Source directly. Think farmers' markets and community-supported agriculture (CSA) boxes. Grocery shopping this way can increase traceability and reduce the likelihood of fraud because your products touch fewer hands. The saying "Know your farmer, know your food" applies to food from the sea as well: Know your fisherman, know your food. Sign up for a community-supported fishery box (search at *localcatch.org*). When eating out, support restaurants that grow or raise their own ingredients (a practice also known as "vertical integration") or that source directly themselves. For instance, you can opt for restaurants participating in programs like Dock to Dish, which is all about the concept of restaurant-supported fisheries. In direct-sourcing models, traceability is high, sustainability is central, and the opportunity to try a wider variety of foods can be exciting as a diner. These programs are supply-driven, flipping the script from the usual demand-driven model. This improves earnings for local farmers and fishermen who no longer have to sell through middlemen.

23

THE GREAT PROTEIN MYTH

E nough with the bender. That is, the years-long bender of beef jerky chewing, whey powder slugging, power bar chomping, and otherwise fixating on our daily acquisition of protein. This national obsession stems quite understandably from a trio of sub-myths, which together I call the Great Protein Myth. Let's debunk them one by one.

WE THINK WE NEED MORE PROTEIN THAN WE DO.

The recommended daily protein intake for a healthy adult is 46 grams for women and 56 grams for men. For context, you can easily get 27 grams of protein from half a chicken breast, 20 grams of protein from a serving of Greek yogurt, 15 from a serving of black beans, 6 from an egg, and 3 from a handful of almonds. Protein malnutrition is a serious problem for millions of people around the globe, but not for the average adult in developed countries like the United States.

WE GET A LOT MORE PROTEIN THAN WE THINK.

Adult males in the United States eat about 100 grams of protein per day, according to a 2015 analysis of data from the National Health and Nutrition Examination Survey. That's almost twice the recommended amount. Females consume less than males do on average but still greatly exceed the necessary amount each day. (The two main exceptions—the only groups more likely to need more protein than they're eating—are teenage girls and the elderly.)

Going overboard on protein is a big waste of your time, energy, money, and calories. Since meat in particular is an environmentally inefficient source of food (see page 191), doing so is also a big waste of our collective water and land. Our excess demand for animal protein sucks up a heck of a lot of the earth's natural resources while emitting tons of greenhouse gases. The excess also means robbing yourself of the room in your diet to eat what most people are actually lacking—namely, whole grains and produce. And don't get me started on powdery protein supplements. Talk about money down the drain. Not to mention the taste. Blech.

There can also be long-term risks in consuming too much protein. Most notably, high-protein diets have been tied to

THE PARIS CLIMATE AGREEMENT

The United States is the only country of the 195 United Nations members worldwide to withdraw from the Paris agreement on climate change that took place in 2015. The UN set a goal to keep the average rise in global temperatures to no more than 2 degrees Celsius, or 3.6 degrees Fahrenheit, compared with the levels before the Industrial Revolution. That zone is an irreversible tipping point we want to collectively head off. It's the only way to avoid suffering from the most catastrophic disasters of global warming—from super-extreme weather events and unsafe heat and drought to lack of drinking water, and ultimately, political upheaval and warfare over scarce natural resources critical to human survival. To fully appreciate how much of an outlier the United States is on this issue, consider that only two other nations originally did not join this commonsense accord, which is backed by heaps of science: Syria and Nicaragua. The former because of being engulfed in years of catastrophic civil war and being too busy racking up human rights violations, the latter because the target in the agreement wasn't ambitious *enough*. (Nicaragua is a global leader in renewable energy.)

higher rates of cancer later in life. This could be because eating a lot of protein often means eating a lot of meat (at least in the United States), and as we'll explore later, there's a link between certain types of meat and cancer risk. It could also be because protein is known for accelerating the replication of cells, something you want only if you're a growing teenager, say, or an elite athlete trying to build muscle.

WE THINK OF PROTEIN AS SYNONYMOUS WITH MEAT.

We all need protein, because it offers amino acids that are the very building blocks of life. It provides our bodies with tissues, skin, bones, and yes, as protein shake lovers know, muscle muscle muscle. Although a steak or chicken sandwich or meal replacement bar might feel like the fastest way to hit your protein count for the day, remember that you don't have to get it all in one sitting; foods' contributions add up throughout the day. Even on a vegan diet, people can easily get 60 to 80 grams of protein throughout the day from foods like beans, nuts, vegetables, and whole grains.

24

THE CONSCIOUS CARNIVORE: FIRST, LESS. THEN, BETTER.

When cattle, goats, and sheep burp, fart, and poop, they emit methane and nitrous oxide. Methane is roughly 30 times more earth warming than carbon dioxide. Nitrous oxide is roughly 290 times more potent than carbon dioxide. Water use is sky-high for livestock, as is land use for not just raising animals but growing their feed, edging out land to grow other crops that are often more nutritious and could be eaten directly. Not to mention cutting down forests (which store carbon) to make way for more pastureland. This activity currently occupies an area the size of both North and South America *combined*. All together, the whole operation of feeding, raising, slaughtering, and transporting livestock accounts for more greenhouse gas emissions than the entire transportation sector—every plane, train, and automobile combined. These are some of the reasons why we should eat less meat. And less red meat in particular.

But there's more. Those who work in the industrial livestock industry or live nearby are exposed to toxic gases—from ammonia to hydrogen sulfide—released from the waste of factory farms. The human health effects range from the direct impacts—children raised near these "farms," more appropriately dubbed confined animal feeding operations, or CAFOs, are more likely to develop asthma, for example—to the indirect climate change impact these farms incur: extreme weather events and flooding → contaminated water and the spread of disease → disproportionate health burden on low-income families.

AFTER LESS MEAT COMES BETTER MEAT. WHAT COUNTS?

There's a trope in my line of work that when you ask children where their steak comes from, they'll say "the supermarket." Because animal flesh comes to us wrapped in cellophane, the act of consuming it is deeply disconnected from the reality that it came from an animal, and at a high environmental cost.

After learning about the litany of problems that livestock production creates for not just the environment but our own welfare, can we really believe in such a thing as a "conscious carnivore"? I say yes, absolutely. Especially because the vast majority of Americans are meat eaters. And I'd guess that most of us intend to remain so.

The problems stem from one key issue: In the industrial model, efficiency trumps all. "All" means the health of the environment, the communities, and the animals that become food. Their overcrowded living conditions in turn further damage the health of the human population as a whole. In treating animals raised for food as little widgets in an assembly line, with the goal of getting as much sellable meat per animal in as little time as possible, growth hormones and all the wrong types of feed are doled out like candy on Halloween. Unlike more nutritious pasture-based diets, this combination works great for fattening up livestock quickly—and pretty much nothing else.

So, better meat comes from animals *not* treated this way. Better meat comes from animals not fed corn all their lives, or raised in CAFOs, or routinely given antibiotics important to human medicine, or pumped with hormones to make them grow faster.

There's a lot to juggle, so here's my list of four practical things you can reasonably do to enjoy meat with a relatively clear conscience:

DO A LOT LESS HARM BY PAYING A LITTLE BIT MORE.
See page 146 for which labels to look for to know you're getting the "better" you deserve. Or, if you have a legitimate farmers' market or responsible butcher shop near you, or a grocery store that has strong animal welfare standards, get your meat there. It will likely be free of all the things that do you, animals, and the planet harm.

EAT LOW ON THE FOOD CHAIN.
The protein sources that are most environmentally concerning are ruminant forms of red meat, as described—beef, lamb, and goat. Trading down from beef to turkey in your sandwich can make a big difference. It's also better for your health in the long run. Ditto for picking tofu instead of chicken in your Chipotle burrito or Chinese takeout—or switching your weekend breakfast routine from bacon and waffles to scrambled eggs and waffles. For the full comparison, check out the World Resources Institute's Protein Scorecard: *wri.org/shiftingdiets*.

EAT IT WHOLE, AND EAT THE WHOLE THING.
Whole cuts of meat are far better for your health than processed meats. Avoid waste by eating nose to tail, which means using every part of each animal that's slaughtered. Buying from your farmers' market or other small-scale producers or butchers—online or in your neighborhood—can help you find those who practice whole-animal butchery.

IN THE FUTURE, CONSIDER LAB-GROWN MEAT.
"Fifty years hence, we shall escape the absurdity of growing a whole chicken in order to eat the breast or wing by growing these parts separately under a suitable medium." This quote from Winston Churchill in 1931 was prescient. Though

lab-grown fare is still in its infancy as far as commercially available products, its future looks favorable. Also known as "cultured meat," "cultivated meat," "cell-based meat," and "clean meat" (it seeks to be the "clean energy" of the meat world), this is meat that comes from animal cells. They get cultured in a laboratory and molded into the shape and function of traditional forms of meat, from burger patties and chicken nuggets to fillets of fish and pieces of duck. Although it can sound a little creepy, the numbers are compelling: This newfangled method could involve up to 96 percent less water, 99 percent less land, and up to 96 percent fewer greenhouse gases compared with conventional meat production (according to a major environmental impact study done by researchers at University of Oxford and the University of Amsterdam in 2011).

Long term, we still need a culture shift to bring us collectively to think of at least beef like we do lobster—a special-occasion treat, an indulgence. But from my perspective, just as electric cars are a stepping-stone away from our overreliance on single-occupancy vehicles, clean meat offers a promising short-term bridge toward easing us off our diets' current overreliance on red meat.

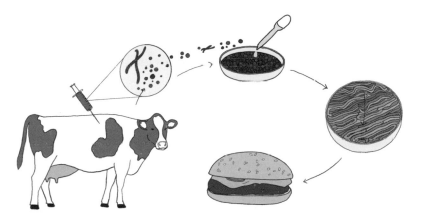

25

THE CONSCIOUS CARNIVORE: ANIMAL WELFARE EDITION

I n a nation that spends innumerable hours a year watching cat videos and pampers its dogs with plush beds and toys, we treat chickens and pigs and cows in ways we would *never* treat felines and canines. Or pet birds for that matter. And then, we eat the animals we just did all that awful stuff to.

For conscious carnivores, it helps to be aware of the "Five Freedoms," which is considered the gold standard for animal welfare. Since it was first proposed in the United Kingdom decades ago, this framework has been widely adopted by groups such as the American Society for the Prevention of Cruelty to Animals that are committed to the fair treatment of animals under human care. The Five Freedoms are:

* freedom from hunger and thirst,

* freedom from discomfort—meaning to be sheltered and given enough space to move and rest comfortably,

* freedom from pain, injury, or disease—meaning to be treated expeditiously in the latter two cases,

* freedom from fear and distress—meaning given conditions that don't cause psychological suffering, and

* freedom *to* express the normal behaviors that a given species would exhibit in nature, like walking around or pecking or grazing.

The global population of livestock consists of approximately 19.6 billion chickens, 1.9 billion sheep and goats, 1.4 billion cattle, and 980 million pigs. For these food-producing animals, there's much agreement among NGOs and advocacy groups that agribusiness producers should be required to comply with the following policies to ensure that at least *most* of these freedoms are met *most* of the time:

* Pregnant sows in hog-breeding operations should not be kept in gestation crates, which confine them during their pregnancy, preventing them from walking, turning, or interacting with other pigs.

* Egg-laying hens should not be raised in battery cages, which inhibit movement by restricting each chicken to a space smaller than a single piece of printer paper—for their entire lives!

* Beyond being able to move around, animals should ideally be given access to the outdoors, preferably pasture.

* For animals that are restricted to the indoors or to feedlots (enclosed spaces where livestock get fattened up before slaughter), housing should be as comfortable as possible. This includes things like shade to protect them from the sun, and fresh air in buildings along with adequate lighting and clean bedding.

* Chickens should be bred more slowly so they don't become so heavy that they can't support their own weight.

* Animals should not be raised with the nontherapeutic use of antibiotics that are medically important to humans. Because the unhygienic conditions of confined

animal feeding operations (CAFOs) boost the likelihood of disease spreading, animals are often given prophylactic antibiotics. Reducing the use of antibiotics in the meat supply can help preserve our collective ability to fight life-threatening bacteria.

How can you tell whether these practices were followed? Choose meat from animals raised without the use of antibiotics, eggs that at the very least come from cage-free chickens, and products with the top three third-party certification labels:

* "Animal Welfare Approved"
* "Certified Humane Raised and Handled"
* "Global Animal Partnership (GAP) Certified"

For cows, the "American Grassfed" label is also very strong, though beware of the fact that the term *grass-fed* is not well regulated on meat packaging. For details see "The Grass-Fed Question" on page 100; for the full breakdown of third-party labels on stuff that comes from animals, see "Stickers to Know" on page 146.

Also, look for farmers and ranchers who raise animals as part of diversified farms, meaning that one type of animal is not the only thing they've got going. Raising animals in concert with other plants and animals makes a big difference, particularly when managed grazing is used, which, thanks to the way cattle fertilize and stir up soil as they forage, means you can actually capture carbon in the soil (though it doesn't offset the methane emitted by those gassy ruminants).

Not to be overlooked is the human cost of industrial livestock production. The worker safety issues, repetitive-stress injuries, grueling hours, and low wages suffered by slaughterhouse workers—which for many Americans were first revealed in the book *Fast Food Nation*—are enough to turn off the appetites of even the most fervent meat eater. To my knowledge, there is not currently a widely available third-party label verifying better labor conditions. The Agricultural Justice Project has launched a label, "Food Justice Certified," whose standards are considered highly meaningful by Consumer Reports, but so far only a small number of farms and producers have earned the certification, so you're unlikely to see it in stores. For now, at least be aware that one more reason to opt out of factory-farmed meat with your grocery dollars is the incredibly inhumane working conditions for people in meat and poultry packing and processing.

26

THE GRASS-FED QUESTION

Not to beat a dead horse, er, cow, but the only sustainable way that a growing population can eat animal-based foods is to eat less of them. In the "First, less. Then, better" equation, we covered "better" for animals, workers, and the planet, so now we turn to the unique case of grass-fed cattle, which is about those things too, but also, importantly, about the impact it has on us.

Ruminant animals—again, such as cattle, sheep, and goats—are not meant to eat grains. Their digestive systems were designed for the way they have eaten from time immemorial, which is to say on pasture. Grass. The stuff that gets stuck in your soccer cleats and offers summer employment for the neighbor kid with a mower. When cows eat grains, soy, and corn, they get fat faster (the goal of CAFOs, after all), but their gut microbiomes get totally hijacked. This, in turn, throws off the usual fermentation that would occur in their stomachs to convert grass and hay into nutrients. Instead, you're left with a bunch of cows craving wagonloads of Rolaids. As a result, they get sick more often and require more antibiotics. Bad news all around.

By contrast, cattle that are pasture-raised get to move about and graze as they are naturally inclined to do. They burn more calories since they get more exercise; grass has fewer calories and more nutrients, so the product—the meat that you then put into *your* body—has fewer calories and more nutrients. In particular, it has more omega-3s, healthy fats that are found in grass.

One last selling point: Many people who try grass-fed beef like that it tastes purer, gamey, and even mineral-y. There's an emerging idea around the terroir of grass-fed beef. Much like the joy of savoring wines from different regions—detecting that a pinot noir from Oregon has different characteristics than a pinot noir from Burgundy, France—you can start to think of the unique opportunity to taste the difference among cattle raised in different parts of the country: On the steep and foggy California coast, cattle are eating different types of grasses compared with those raised, say, on the flat and sunny grasslands of Colorado.

It remains to be seen whether the potential to capture carbon in the soil by grazing cattle on pasture can essentially cancel out their high methane emissions. Under optimal grazing scenarios, it appears this neutrality is at least possible, but only more research will clarify how replicable these scenarios are across the growing grass-fed industry. Some initial studies also suggest that adding seaweed to cattle feed can dramatically cut methane emissions, since it can alter their gut composition.

WHAT TO LOOK FOR WHEN BUYING GRASS-FED BEEF

The USDA has in the past standardized the term *grass fed* for beef. However, it has revoked its label standard, acknowledging widespread confusion about its meaning. It continues to regulate the use of the label on beef, though rather meagerly. The FDA does not have a standard definition for the term on dairy products. So, that term alone does not provide great assurance of how much of an animal's life it was allowed to graze for, or what percentage of its overall diet came from grass.

Bottom line: You're best off with a third-party-verified stamp. According to Consumer Reports, two of the most meaningful labels for grass-fed products are "American Grassfed" and "PCO Certified 100% GrassFed":

* "American Grassfed." This means the cow—or goat, lamb, or other animal—really ate only grass or forage (or hay in winter, which is dried grass). The exception is when they (rightfully) had milk from their mother before they were weaned. Certified by the American Grassfed Association, it also means animals were raised only on pasture.

* "PCO Certified 100% GrassFed." This label applies only to beef and dairy products from cows, so it means the cattle really ate only grass or forage (or hay in winter). It's provided by the Pennsylvania Certified Organic organization and is a reminder that the healthy diets of *dairy* cows involve many of the similar benefits as those of beef cattle.

To sum up, grass-fed red meat and dairy products are good—because they're more nutritious, lower in calories, and better for the animals—but not great, because the net greenhouse gas emissions aren't yet clear, and you're still eating red meat and dairy products.

27

WHY FISH AND SEAFOOD ARE WORTH YOUR WHILE

When it comes to consuming life under water, there are *a lot* of issues to contend with.

IS IT WORTH IT?
To cut to the chase: Given the abundance of other foods available to most people in the United States, most of us don't *need* to eat fish and seafood for survival—or even for optimal nutrition. As with milk, if all the associated production problems are enough to make you throw your hands up and ask whether it's really worth the trouble to buy the darn thing, the answer in both cases is that it may not be. And that's perfectly fine.

But fish are packed with things we want in our bodies— protein and vitamins and minerals. They also have nutrients that are somewhat hard to obtain elsewhere in the diet, such as omega-3 fatty acids, a type of healthy polyunsaturated fat, of which fish are the best source out there. Omega-3s are essential for helping cell membranes form, and yet our bodies don't produce them on their own, so we have to get them from food. As you may have seen on labels or supplements, EPA and DHA in particular (two types of omega-3s whose full names are incomprehensible) have been tied to lower risk of heart attacks and strokes, and to the development of the brain and nervous system in infants. For these reasons, pregnant women are encouraged to eat certain types of fish up to twice a week, and at least one good source of omega-3s per day. Adults more generally are encouraged to eat fish twice a week. Numerous studies have confirmed the health-promoting powers of the Mediterranean diet, and omega-3s from fatty fish like sardines and salmon are a major part of the diet's strong merits.

THERE ARE AT LEAST THREE BRIGHT SPOTS IN THE QUEST TO UP YOUR OMEGA-3 INTAKE:

1   You don't need to eat that much to reap the health benefits.

2   Many of the oily fish low on the food chain are packed full of the good stuff without having bad stuff; humble anchovies, in the cute little can, give you 500 milligrams of omega-3s, which is the daily recommended amount for most people.

3   Foods other than fish contain EPA and DHA—just in smaller amounts, like chicken and eggs—and beans, nuts, seeds, fruits, and vegetables have alpha-linolenic acid, the third type of omega-3 fatty acid, which your body converts to EPA and DHA. By eating a variety of foods, you can gradually rack up a decent log of omega-3s without eating fish.

WHAT ABOUT MERCURY?

The biggest concern with methylmercury—a toxic substance found in some seafood, especially in waters near industrial pollution—is damage to the brain and nervous systems of developing fetuses. Wait, aren't those the same parts that benefit from DHA and EPA intake? Why, yes indeed. Pretty critical parts of the body, you'd have to say. Hence all this real estate I'm dedicating to duking out the two sides of the argument.

What's mercury doing in our rivers and lakes and oceans? It can get there naturally, from volcanoes, or from man-made causes—most significantly coal-fired power plants, which make up a significant amount of US mercury emissions into the atmosphere.

Although current mercury intake isn't a threat for most adults, those with elevated risk are pregnant women, women

BIGGER FISH CONTAIN LARGER, MORE CONCENTRATED AMOUNTS OF MERCURY.

who might become pregnant, women nursing infants, and small children. These groups most definitely should avoid the following types of fish:

king mackerel // marlin // orange roughy // shark // swordfish // tilefish (also called golden snapper or golden bass) // bigeye tuna

In general, large predator fish are riskier from a mercury standpoint because toxicity concentrates as you go higher up the food chain. The fat and muscles of fish absorb mercury from contaminated waters in which they swim. Predator fish eat lots of smaller fish, so higher amounts build up in their bodies, whereas fish low on the food chain subsist mostly on teeny-tiny plants and animals called plankton. Examples of these small fatty fish are herring, anchovies, and sardines, which happen to be rich in omega-3s.

Pregnant women: Because of the importance of consuming DHA and EPA for your growing baby's brain development and nervous system, the risks of not eating fish are much higher than the risks of mercury contamination. There are far more types of fish that are safe and even really good for you to eat than there are types that are harmful. So, know the main ones to avoid for mercury contamination—king mackerel, marlin, orange roughy, shark, swordfish, tilefish, and bigeye tuna—and otherwise, enjoy. Your baby will thank you.

FOOD SAFETY AND ALLERGIES

Foodborne illness from seafood is unfortunately quite common. It can come from improper handling during cleaning, transportation, storage, or processing, or from the increased risk of viruses when eating raw fish or shellfish. Although delicious in forms from sushi to oysters (both of which I personally love), the safety questions around raw fish and seafood are nothing to take lightly. The FDA website has a helpful resource called "Fresh and Frozen Seafood: Selecting and Serving It Safely." Their tips include the following:

* Avoid purchasing frozen seafood packages with lots of frost or ice crystals. That could indicate thawing and refreezing, which can spoil fish and seafood.

* Store raw fish and seafood in the refrigerator if you'll use it within two days of purchase; otherwise store it in the freezer.

* Once it's cooked and ready to serve, keep cold seafood cold (on ice) and keep hot seafood hot, especially if either will be out for more than two hours.

And if you're having people over for a party or dinner, ask ahead about fish and shellfish allergies, because both are among the top eight food allergens for Americans.

28

SUSTAINABILITY AT SEA: A PRIMER

ecause of overfishing, approximately 90 percent of the top underwater predators have been wiped out. Consider bluefin tuna from the Pacific Ocean, which was recently estimated at *3 percent* of its original volume, or North Atlantic cod, which dried up altogether. All in the span of just the past few decades. (The book *Cod*, by Mark Kurlansky, gives the full saga.) And we're sadly on track to keep eradicating many of the remaining species over the coming years. So, if there aren't enough fish left in the ocean, shouldn't we avoid eating fish entirely? There are actually plenty of great ways to enjoy fish and seafood that are raised or caught using responsible practices. You just have to know what to look for—and what to look out for.

Aside from overfishing, the other big concerns with fish, seafood, and the planet are habitat damage and bycatch, which occurs when marine life other than the species targeted by a fishing operation (such as dolphins and turtles) get hauled aboard a boat with the nets and lines, only to then be tossed back into the sea dead or halfway there.

To cut to the chase: **The best way to ensure that your seafood is sustainable is to consult Seafood Watch, from the Monterey Bay Aquarium.** Free downloadable guides are available for all fifty states, as is a mobile phone app so you can reference the go-to information whenever and wherever you find yourself making decisions about fish and seafood, whether farmed or wild caught.

What it means: Seafood Watch uses a three-part rating scheme: "Best" (labeled green) means the fish are caught or farmed using methods that are minimally damaging to marine life and environments. They exist in abundant supply. "Good" (labeled yellow) means they're fine for you to buy, but some issues have been identified with how the products are caught or farmed. "Avoid" (labeled red) means they're caught or farmed in harmful ways and/or that they are overfished. The criteria behind these categories are based on the optimal locations of origin, species type, aquaculture methods, or fishing equipment.

What it doesn't mean: That fair prices were necessarily given to the fishermen or fisherwomen, or that those individuals caught the fish under humane work conditions. For the latter, Seafood Watch developed a separate Seafood Slavery Risk Tool.

Why it's legit: By far the most comprehensive, trusted, and widely recognized certifier of sustainable seafood on the market in the United States, it is used by both retailers and restaurants to ensure fish and shellfish choices that do not deplete certain species or degrade oceans or waterways.

When eating out, search the Seafood Watch website (*seafoodwatch.org*) for restaurants that have partnered with the organization, as you can rest assured that *everything* those restaurants serve is free of items from the "Avoid" list. Staff at these restaurants may also receive training around sustainable seafood issues. For cooking at home, you can search for their retail partners, such as Whole Foods Market, which means they have committed to selling only environmentally responsible choices, at least for a certain period of time.

Seafood Watch draws attention to the following concerns when evaluating whether a given type of sea creature is "sustainable."

Health of fish populations. In measuring the health of a fish stock, what counts as "enough"? It generally means the population can repopulate itself. That means not fishing faster than it takes for that to occur, as often happens with commercial fishing practices under business as usual.

Who gets to decide? That's where responsible fisheries management comes in, with management agencies setting official catch limits to put fishermen in a given area on clear notice and equal footing. Given the scale of the overfishing that has already happened, the extent of the oversight needed varies by location and species. Some species that are depleted but not completely wiped out simply need time to recover, and for that, we have Marine Protected Areas. You can think of them like state or national parks. They're designed to lure fish into propagation mode, so the full ecosystem can rejuvenate. Surely the place that gets the gold star for responsible fisheries management is Alaska's Bristol Bay. The approach there is rigorous, the waters are pristine, the habitats are healthy, and the salmon stocks are at record highs.

Type of fishing gear used. Industrial fishing boats use imprecise gear—gillnets, longlines, bottom trawls—that drag up all kinds of life other than their target catch, from sharks to sea turtles, and even innocent birds flocking around the boats that get caught in the tangle. That's because some of these contraptions can span *fifty miles*. Bottom trawling, along with giant metal baskets called dredges, drag not only through the water but along the bottom of the ocean floor. That sweeps up creatures it shouldn't, like clear-cutting a forest, while also disrupting habitat—coral reefs, sponges, and the homes and food sources for marine life who live there. This method is also about three times as damaging as non-trawling in terms of greenhouse gas emissions. Using traps and pots to catch prawns instead, for example, can reduce bycatch and seafloor damage. These are some of the reasons why Seafood Watch's rating system includes the type of gear involved. The better options are hook-and-line tools, which allow fishermen to more rapidly release bycatch rather than kill them.

Illegal fishing. An estimated one-fifth of fish and seafood caught worldwide is illegal, unreported, or unregulated. These seedy practices can result in both depletion of species and damage to marine ecosystems.

WHAT'S A CONSCIOUS EATER TO DO?

* Use the Seafood Watch tools for both grocery and restaurant decisions in order to focus on sustainability. Ideally, cross-reference their guides with two handy consumer tools for mercury levels and omega-3 content. The **Environmental Working Group (EWG)'s Consumer Guide to Seafood** has an interactive tool to personalize a seafood list to your unique profile, as well as a simple cheat sheet of their "best bets," meaning those fish are very high in omega-3s and low in mercury and come from sustainable sources. Their best bets are salmon and sardines, mussels and Atlantic mackerel, and rainbow trout. Their "avoid" list consists of king mackerel, marlin, orange roughy, shark, swordfish, and tilefish (six of the same ones to avoid for mercury alone). The **Environmental Defense Fund's "Seafood Selector"** lets you filter by just eco-friendly or eco-friendly + healthy, and then to sort by "best choices" down to "worst choices." They also provide a sushi-specific guide. Their best choices are wild Alaskan salmon, albacore tuna, and Pacific sardines from the United States and Canada, canned salmon, and sablefish (also called black cod).

SUSTAINABLE SEAFOOD CHEAT SHEET

These species are rated by Environmental Working Group as coming from sustainable sources and being high in omega-3s, low in mercury.

BEST BETS
* Atlantic mackerel
* mussels
* rainbow trout
* salmon
* sardines

AVOID
* king mackerel
* marlin
* orange roughy
* shark
* swordfish
* tilefish

* If you're unsure where an item stands in Seafood Watch's book, rely on labels from third-party certifiers. **For everything wild caught, the label to look for is the Marine Stewardship Council (MSC)'s blue fish label.** You can find it at the fish counter and on fish products, supplements (like fish oil), and even pet food. Based in the United Kingdom, MSC developed the first certification for wild, sustainable seafood. To be certified, fisheries must meet twenty-eight carefully audited criteria across three key principles that make up their definition of *sustainable*: fish caught from stocks whose populations are thriving, in ways that minimally impact the surrounding environment, and from a region where fishery management is up to snuff. No wonder Monterey Bay Aquarium endorses them, since their standards are clearly aligned.

For farmed fish, look for Aquaculture Stewardship Council (ASC) certification. Their strict standards minimize the impact of fish farming on water quality and surrounding habitats and marine life, require responsible disease management, and enforce fair wages and good working conditions for workers in the industry, including prohibiting both child labor and forced labor.

* Eat low on the food chain, i.e., small fish.

* Speak up! Whether you're buying fish from a small local purveyor or big-box supermarket, or ordering it at a fast food chain or fine-dining restaurant, ask questions about origin, Seafood Watch rating, wild versus farmed, food safety measures, and so on. The more seafood buyers are pressured by consumers for this level of transparency, the more likely suppliers will feel pressured to meet those demands.

29

FARMED FISH: YAY OR NAY?

You can think of a typical fish farm much like a cattle feedlot: Too many creatures crammed into too little space and fed too much sub-optimal feed, making them too sick and fat. Tens of thousands of rapidly growing fish swarming amid net pens or ponds. Ergo, fish farmers relying on the usual Band-Aid solutions—antibiotics, pesticides, and other chemicals—which round out the CAFO (confined animal feeding operation) analogy by similarly contributing to antibiotic resistance and environmental degradation. But instead of in factory farms on land, it all transpires under water.

MORE REASONS *NOT* TO EAT FARMED FISH:

Fish out of water. It's harder to maintain a hard border, so to speak, when you're housing living things in a body of water. Imagine large cages made of netting, floating offshore. Inevitably, fish escape, at least in the case of farmed salmon, which is a particularly problematic type of fish farming. This can result in the spread of disease as well as fish acting as invasive species in these waters where they don't belong. They can even mate with wild fish, which can mess with the genetics of the wild population.

Less healthy fish. When fish are confined, they're less active. The result is fish who are fatter than their wild cousins, who get tons of exercise and live off small fish and krill (little crustaceans). For us, this means farmed salmon develop up to three times the saturated fat of wild salmon (much like the comparison for grass-fed beef). This high saturated fat content is caused by what the farmed salmon are fed, which is a face-scrunching blend of pellets made from fish oil and fish meal (derived from larger fish), soy and wheat, and sundry by-products of slaughtered farm animals. Excuse me, but what's a fish doing eating a cow!? Talk about Frankenfood.

PCBs. Unfortunately, methylmercury isn't the only toxic chemical that finds its way into our fish supply. After years of agricultural and industrial uses, chemicals including polychlorinated biphenyls, or PCBs, were banned decades ago because of suspected ties to cancer and skin and liver harm. But their waste streams have left residual contamination in waters that fish inhabit. Though reports vary, several studies have found that PCB levels are much higher in farm-raised salmon, which is likely caused by the way PCBs concentrate in oils and fat, which fish meal is high in. Consuming high amounts poses risks during pregnancy and early infancy, and the higher up the food chain a fish is, and the more a fish eats lots of other fish, the more PCBs it's likely to have. If this sounds familiar, it's the same principle of bioaccumulation that puts predator fish at the top of the no-no list for mercury. Unfortunately, fattier fish have more PCBs, and those are the ones at the top of the yes-yes list for omega-3s. (It's exhausting, I know. Believe me!)

Pink dye. Krill are also what give wild salmon its enticing bright pink color. To mimic that color in farmed salmon, artificial coloring is added to feed pellets, which the fish flesh absorbs. Salmon farmers use the dye to get their product to sell, since consumer research shows that almost no one is psyched about eating a fish fillet that's gray. The health effects of the dye are not yet understood, but in the interest of transparency, many consumers want to know.

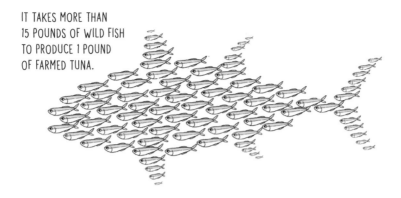

IT TAKES MORE THAN 15 POUNDS OF WILD FISH TO PRODUCE 1 POUND OF FARMED TUNA.

Depleting wild fish stocks for feed. Producing fish feed is extremely inefficient. It takes more than 15 pounds of wild fish to produce 1 pound of farmed tuna. This practice ravages stocks of certain "forage fish" (anchovies, herring, menhaden) to make fish meal and fish oil to feed the fish whose wild stocks you're supposedly offsetting by enhancing the total supply. Not a great trade.

Environmental impact. Spillage or intentional discharge of the toxic chemicals used for the aforementioned crowded net pens or ponds, not to mention waste, can damage surrounding waters and the life within them.

STILL, BEFORE WE EXILE THE FOOD CATEGORY ENTIRELY, HERE'S AN IMPORTANT CAVEAT:

Not all food that comes from aquaculture (the business of fish farming) is the same.

- Bivalves—mussels, clams, scallops, and oysters—are farmed more responsibly. They're not carnivores, so they don't require wild fish. Moreover, because shellfish are filter feeders, water quality is often improved as a result of their taking up residence.

- Farmed fish systems that use recirculated, treated water for fish in tanks (on land) generally don't negatively affect wild fish and their habitats. Examples of species routinely raised in this way in the United States are Arctic char, catfish, cobia, tilapia, and trout, according to Seafood Watch.

In judging a given food choice, you always have to ask, "As opposed to what?" If you're considering not eating farmed fish because you're worried about the dye or other environmental issues, but then you go and eat a burger instead, that's not exactly a smart swap.

WHAT TO DO

* In the case of salmon, eat wild only, and either consider it a special-occasion treat, since it costs a pretty penny when fresh, or look for affordable ways to enjoy it more regularly, from frozen to canned. Skip the farmed stuff.

* If you do pick farmed salmon, check Seafood Watch for not only the best method and type of salmon but the country of origin; according to Oceana, Chile's salmon farms use an enormous quantity of antibiotics, whereas those in Norway use hardly any.

* Eat the feed. Small fish like anchovies and herring are used to feed farmed fish like tuna. Instead, eat those little guys. As with eating plant-based foods in place of animals they've been fed to, eating the feed signals to the market that "feed" is also valuable human food.

* For farmed fish and seafood, again, go lower on the food chain (think shellfish). The carbon footprint of mussels, for example, is thirty times less than that of beef.

* Opt for fish species that do well onshore, such as Arctic char, catfish, cobia, tilapia, and trout.

30

SHRIMP + SLAVERY = ONE HOT MESS

n the United States, it's common to think of slavery as a scar
of the past, a dark regression in an otherwise gradual march
toward civic enlightenment, during which humans treated
other humans as sub-human. Enslaved people were forced to
work against their will, and their basic needs, such as safe living quarters, rest, food, and water, were withheld—often while
they were being subjected to violent physical and psychological abuse.

Unfortunately, this reality is not merely an abomination
from history. As many have been shocked to learn, slavery has
been rampant recently in the seafood industry. It is primarily
a problem in Southeast Asia, and especially in the shrimp sector of Thailand. Not only men and women but children have
suffered under unconscionable work conditions in the name
of bringing seafood to tables and pet bowls, including ours in
the United States. The most alarming case involved the largest shrimp farm on the planet, Charoen Pokphand (CP) Foods,
based in Thailand. It has been supplying most major supermarkets, including the top four globally, Carrefour, Costco,
Tesco, and Walmart.

Often the workers are migrants who get taken by traffickers
to serve in what the *New York Times* called "floating labor camps."
Work without wages for years at a time. Beatings. Even murder.
No matter how hot or cold, light or dark, stormy or calm, boat
captains and crew masters demand long hours, meaning almost

no sleep. Often there's just one meal per day, of questionable nutritional quality and food safety.

Sadly, seafood is by no means the only sector of the food and agriculture supply chain plagued by inhumane work practices. An estimated 21 million people are victims of forced labor around the world, and 3.5 million of them work in some form of agriculture (which includes fishing and forestry). Although the problem is much worse in developing countries, neither the United States nor Europe is entirely virtuous. In 2016, the nonprofit group KnowTheChain reported that one in twenty farmworkers in the United States is working against his or her own will. Most of them are migrant workers from Mexico, Guatemala, and Haiti, the report says, and they receive little or no pay.

Fishing is particularly susceptible to shady behavior, though, because once a boat has left a harbor and dipped past the horizon, no one is watching. Part of the reason this is so problematic in Southeast Asian waters is the larger issue of "illegal, unreported, and unregulated" (IUU) fishing—the designations of suspicious fishing. It's estimated that one in five fish and seafood products worldwide is IUU. What's on the list of illegal practices? Taking more fish than is permitted. Taking the wrong size, or taking them in the wrong season. Catching fish from another country's waters without consent. And slavery. Definitely not legal—anywhere in the world.

After consumers, restaurateurs, retailers, and government officials were left shell-shocked when an exposé by *The Guardian* first came out in 2014, we quickly yearned for solutions. Headlines like "How to find shrimp that's not produced by slave labor in Thailand" certainly caught my attention in the months afterward, as did "Thai seafood: Are the prawns on your plate still fished by slaves?" years later. Well into 2018, journalists and NGOs continued to unearth more disturbing details while keeping tabs on the issue. Tragically, as *The Guardian* reported in 2018, despite pledges from the Thai government to clamp down, many of the problems have persisted—from migrant workers sold like goods and subjected to unfathomable working conditions to physical abuse and the injustice of not being paid at all.

In 2014, Barack Obama established the Presidential Task Force on Combating IUU Fishing and Seafood Fraud. Visit *iuufishing.noaa.gov* to see how the action plan is unfolding.

WHAT CAN YOU DO? ABOVE ALL, INSIST ON TRACEABILITY.

There are several ways to make sure what you're buying can be traced to legitimate fisheries whose practices have been verified.

* The Marine Stewardship Council blue eco-label that applies to sustainability standards also verifies the specific fishery where fish and seafood are sourced, and therefore that they're worthy of certification. But remember, this is for wild-caught fish and seafood only.

* For farmed products, the Aquaculture Stewardship Council's label is a good way to verify strict standards for not only sustainability but also social responsibility and traceability.

* With Seafood Watch already having established itself as the go-to guide for sustainable seafood, used by millions of people each year, it was fitting—and much needed—that the Monterey Bay Aquarium helped launch a database called the Seafood Slavery Risk Tool. (You can find it at *seafoodslaveryrisk.org*.) Although this feature is primarily

aimed at a business audience, you can still use it to learn about the human rights track record of a fishery before you buy.

* If no third-party labels are available and you're unsure about a product you're considering buying at a grocery store or restaurant, ask questions. "Where is the farmed shrimp from exactly? Was the fish on your menu caught legally?" Transparency is not merely the modern currency of the retail and restaurant worlds—it is your right.

* Check for country of origin. The majority of shrimp we eat in the United States is imported, so you've got to be vigilant. Clearly, shrimp from Thailand remains untrustworthy, so I'd avoid it altogether until we can be sure it's free of human rights violations. Shrimp from US sources—North Carolina, Louisiana, Florida, Texas, and Alaska—are safer choices. Surprised to see how much more those options may cost? This is a reflection of how artificially low the prices have been set for shrimp from ill-gotten sources—stealing wages, well-being, and dignity from the people laboring to get it to us.

Being a conscious eater doesn't mean forking over your entire paycheck to support only the top-of-the-line products or precious artisanal foods. But it does mean being aware of the true cost of food—and doing everything in your power and within your means to adjust your expectations and weekly shopping habits accordingly.

31

EGGS & CHOLESTEROL: WHAT GIVES?

Eggs are beloved by many people, in many cultures. So it was a pretty big downer when the nutrition police told everyone to stop eating them. High cholesterol and heart disease were on the line.

But eggs have since been exonerated. In 2015, one of the biggest headline-makers from the Dietary Guidelines for Americans was that we don't need to worry about dietary cholesterol anymore. It was one big medical "never mind!" The original guidance to avoid eggs had been based on mostly short-term studies, from which the evidence wasn't nearly as strong as that available in recent years. Back then, all three types of fat were locked up together, and only more recently was unsaturated fat proven innocent and released from the slammer, whereas trans fat got shipped off to maximum security with a life sentence, and saturated fat's been kept in the can but at one of those cushy white-collar prisons. In 2015, egg producers surely did a happy dance on farms nationwide. The phrase *put an egg on it* turned up everywhere, as did actual eggs, on pizza to salad, fried rice to avocado toast.

What gives? Why all those years of being told to avoid eggs? Some nomenclature will clarify—a bit.

Cholesterol: Unlike carbs, protein, and fat (the three macro-nutrients), cholesterol is not an energy source but

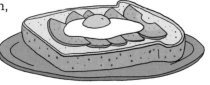

instead helps make cell membranes. These are mega-important wrappers around our nerves. Cholesterol also helps the body produce various hormones as well as vitamin D.

Blood cholesterol. This is the total cholesterol level your doc is referring to after a blood test. It includes LDL (bad, you want it low) and HDL (good, you want it high). When the wrong kinds of lipoproteins—little packages that carry cholesterol through your bloodstream—are overly populous, they clog arteries and can lead to heart attack and stroke. How much of both types you have floating around your body is determined mainly by the types of fat you eat, as well as by sugar intake.

Dietary cholesterol. This is the amount of cholesterol in a food. Only animal-based foods have any. That's because it's made not only by our human bodies but by the bodies of other animals. One egg has about 200 milligrams of cholesterol—among the highest of any foods. And it's all in the yolk. (The rest of your daily intake likely accumulates from small amounts in meat, milk, cheese, and other animal products.) *But it doesn't really matter, because dietary cholesterol only very minimally affects blood cholesterol.* The 2015 Dietary Guidelines for Americans removed dietary cholesterol as a "nutrient of concern," meaning the nutrition community acknowledged that the best available evidence suggested that the previous guidance given for so many years had actually been mistaken. What had likely happened was that researchers knew LDL cholesterol in our blood raises heart disease risk (a correlation they still stand by), so it was only logical to suggest that people steer clear of foods that contained cholesterol. Except that's not how it actually works in the body. As Dr. Walter Willett wrote in his book *Eat, Drink, and Be Healthy,* "No research has ever shown that people who regularly eat eggs have more heart attacks than people who don't eat eggs." Nada. A professor and the former chairman of the Department of Nutrition at the Harvard T. H. Chan School of Public Health, he's speaking from years of careful study, tracking the eating habits of more than 100,000 people at a time. In fact, he's one of the most cited researchers in all areas of science. When asked about a study published in JAMA in 2019 (which sparked headlines suggesting the debate had yet again been reopened), he said the analysis was weak and doesn't change the conclusion based on the overall body of evidence: that essentially there isn't a relationship between the two things. The main exception, and an important one, appears to be people with diabetes, for whom there is a more serious increased risk of heart disease associated with eating eggs too often.

Eggs are packed with vitamins, relatively low in calories, and very low in saturated fat, and they even provide some unsaturated fat. They're also a highly affordable form of protein—especially compared with meat. Plus, as with everything we eat, you have to look at food in terms of the full package of relative goodness it provides, not just through the lens of nutrient-centrism. Eggs are culturally relevant to many cuisines and easy to cook—a hot plate or even a microwave will do. For all these reasons, they can play an important role in supporting food security for low-income families, students living on limited budgets, and many others. Having said this, the recurring question of "as opposed to what" means that although eggs are fine, if the goal is to eat for optimal health, they're a better breakfast choice than bacon or other processed meats, as well as sugary cereal and white bread, but not nearly as good as a breakfast made up of whole grains, nuts, and fruit.

Now that you know that heart health isn't reason to rain on eggs' parade, and you can eat up to an egg a day guilt-free, what else might you factor into the decision to eat them or not? Two main things: First, on the bright side, eggs score high for providing a heavy dose of protein while leaving only a light footprint on the planet, according to the World Resources Institute's Protein Scorecard. Second, on the dark side, beware of animal welfare concerns when buying eggs, because different producers treat egg-laying hens differently, and the status quo isn't pretty.

IN CASE YOU'RE WONDERING . . . 3 BOTTOM LINES ON 3 OTHER EGGS-ISTENTIAL QUESTIONS

1 Brown eggs are no better for you than white ones. The shell color, along with the size, reflects the breed of chicken the egg came from.

2 For most people's health, it doesn't matter if you eat eggs whole or just the whites, unless you're watching calories.

3 In Europe and elsewhere, or if you raise chickens yourself or get them from a farmers' market, eggs don't need refrigeration. This is because eggs have a naturally protective outer layer. Commercially produced eggs in the United States need refrigerating because that layer is power-washed off. This occurs because of USDA concerns about eliminating any dirt on the shell that could pose a food safety risk. Except this practice actually makes the porous shell vulnerable to contamination. Seems ludicrous, if you ask me.

32

THE LAUNDRY LIST
OF EGG LABELS

F rankly, people *do* judge a book by its cover. In the grocery store, you'll see egg cartons swaddled in so many labels, they might remind you of vintage suitcases stamped with alluring stickers of destinations visited. An egg carton may feature depictions of bright rays of sunshine, cherry-red barns, or cartoon images of deliriously happy hens. On price, you see a significant spectrum. The labels range from meaningless to meaningful, with some gray area in between.

THE FOLLOWING LABELS ARE MEANINGLESS—NOTHING BUT MARKETING:

"Natural" // "All-Natural" // "Fresh" // "Farm-Fresh"

"No Hormones." This goes without saying in the egg industry. Hens that lay eggs aren't allowed to be given hormones. All eggs are no-hormone eggs.

"United Egg Producers Certified." This voluntary program looks impressive on a label but acts as the least common denominator for egg producers, nearly all of whom participate. Its standards are technically verified, but those standards are so low, I wouldn't put any stock in the label: Hens are still confined, jam-packed with other hens, and deprived of fresh air and sunlight.

THESE LABELS ARE MEANINGFUL; THE PRACTICES HAVE BEEN VETTED AND ARE WORTH YOUR ATTENTION:

"Animal Welfare Approved." Considered the top animal welfare label on the market by Consumer Reports, this label represents producers who have gone well beyond cage-free or free-range or ensuring appropriate feed. It means animals are given the freedom to engage in their natural behaviors. Egg-laying hens are allowed to walk around, peck for bugs, nest, and so on.

"Certified Humane Raised and Handled." This certification ensures that specific standards have been met for one of the three levels related to eggs—cage-free, free-range, or pasture-raised. If you see this label, you'll also see one of those three designations.

"Global Animal Partnership (GAP) Certified." This is a five-step program tailored to specific species, including egg-laying hens, and is most notably used by Whole Foods Market. Look for these different steps, which have different label colors: Step 1: no cages, crates, or crowding; Step 2: enriched environments (supplying materials—like hay bales and food hung from a string—that encourage their natural behaviors, such as scratching, foraging, pecking, and exploring); Step 3: enhanced outdoor access; Step 4: pasture-centered; Step 5: animal-centered and no physical alterations. Step 5+ means animal-centered and their entire lives are spent on the same farm (except for chickens, which may be transferred right before slaughter). It also means no growth hormones, animal by-products in any species' feed, or antibiotics (except for chickens). This is the highest rating available.

"No Antibiotics." This means egg producers did not add antibiotics to the feed or water of the egg-laying chickens.

"Certified Organic." Carefully regulated by the USDA, organic certification sets specific requirements for what egg-laying hens are fed—the food must be vegetarian and free from pesticides or antibiotics—and how the land they're raised on is treated. So, it's a strong one from environmental and public health standpoints. Where it's not so strong is animal welfare.

For assurance of access to the outdoors or more extensive lifestyle enhancements for the birds, look for the aforementioned animal welfare labels or the more rigorous versions of "pasture-raised" or "free-range," as described below.

THESE LABELS REPRESENT THE VAST GRAY AREA IN BETWEEN MEANINGLESS AND MEANINGFUL—NOT BAD, BUT THE INTENTION-TO-REALITY RATIO IS MURKY:

"Cage-Free." Hens are likely still raised in very confined quarters squished up against each other, and they may or may not be let outdoors. But at least they're not in tiny cages, and in theory they are free to move around and do their usual chicken thing. Cage-free means a lot more when buying eggs—whose hens are indeed most commonly confined to cruelly small cages—than it does when buying chicken, because broilers aren't usually raised in cages to begin with.

"Free-Range" or "Free-Roaming." This one is often interchangeable with "cage-free," except its extra selling point is outdoor access. The problem is that there's no regulatory definition of *free-range*, so in practice the outdoor space could be quite small, and that access might be available to only a fraction of the hens in a given house. It's best if it's attached to a third-party verification for animal welfare standards.

"Pasture-Raised." A fairly good indicator, the term means birds were mostly raised outside and let loose to roam and forage for food. Consider it a notch above free-range and cage-free. That said, it's not enforced by the USDA, so the exact meaning is rather hazy. Your best bet is to trust this claim when it is paired with one of the legit animal welfare labels like "Certified Humane Raised and Handled."

"Vegetarian-Fed." This is fairly straightforward, but the reason it's noteworthy is that a lot of agribusiness involves feeding food animals parts of other animals. Although this issue isn't as relevant in the egg industry as it is in meat and poultry, it can be a reassurance for some shoppers, and especially vegetarian shoppers.

"Omega-3s." This label means the hens' feed included one of the main sources of omega-3 fatty acids—most commonly fish oil, flaxseeds, or flaxseed oil. Although you can indeed add to your daily omega-3 tally this way, the challenge is knowing which type of omega-3 and how much you're getting, since the conversion to human nutrient is unclear on the packaging and not required on the label. These eggs are probably perfectly fine to eat, but can sometimes be a waste of the extra money. You might focus your omega-hunting attentions elsewhere in your diet, such as by eating fish or flaxseed directly.

Finally, pay attention to what the egg carton is made of. Buy eggs whose containers are cardboard, ideally, which is compostable. Second choice is plastic, which is at least recyclable. Never buy eggs in Styrofoam. That material is all-around bad and should be eliminated from use wherever it still manages to turn up.

33

SUPERBUGS AND THE FOOD SUPPLY

A s I write, I've got two buns in the oven. A year before you read these words, I'll be swept to the hospital in a flurry, enduring the greatest pain known to womankind, and put under the care of trained medical professionals. I'm lucky to live in a place where I pretty much trust these people to safely bring two humans into the world while keeping me alive. If it comes down to it, I may require a C-section. That's a major surgery but one conducted with such routine frequency in the United States, most of us don't blink an eye at the prospect.

But what if the drugs used to ensure safe surgeries—or to administer chemotherapy to cancer patients, or to treat an infant's bacterial ear infection—stopped working? This potential "post-antibiotic era" is not a sci-fi movie but a very real scenario that experts predict could mean 10 million people dying each year from antibiotic-resistant bacteria by 2050. That's compared with about 23,000 Americans dying each year from them already. It would mean overtaking cancer as the leading cause of death worldwide. Antibiotics are so essential to public health that it's hard to overstate how reliant we are on them working as intended. Nobody wants to die from a small cut on their hand.

We all agree that we want antibiotics to work. How do we make that happen? The total use of antibiotics, which is currently excessive and has been on the rise for years, must come down in order to preserve their effectiveness.

Of all the antibiotics sold in the United States, just 30 percent are for people (think sinus and ear infections). The rest—70 percent—are for farm animals. Keep in mind that *farm* here is not the Old MacDonald idyll, but rather the industrial farm model. And that's the very root of the problem: If feedlots weren't so overcrowded and unhygienic in the first place, there'd be less inclination to prophylactically pump animals with drugs. The goal among the users is to prevent disease. And until recently, it was also to make animals grow faster, although that's now illegal in the United States. But it's unacceptable to give antibiotics to healthy animals. The only appropriate use is to treat existing infections.

What is antibiotic resistance exactly? When you take an antibiotic to treat an infection caused by disease-causing bacteria, it kills any of those bacteria susceptible to the drug. So, you feel better and stop taking the medication. But some remaining

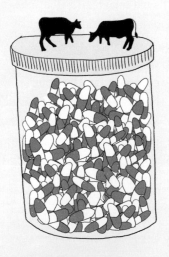

OF ALL THE ANTIBIOTICS SOLD IN THE UNITED STATES, JUST 30 PERCENT ARE FOR PEOPLE. THE OTHER 70 PERCENT ARE FOR FARM ANIMALS.

bacteria in the mix that are already resistant to the drug can now spring forth and multiply. You feel sick again, but when you go to take that antibiotic again, it doesn't work. At the same time, a lot of your good bacteria, responsible for providing your body with immunity to illness, can get killed in the process. Remember the importance of maintaining a healthy mix of beneficial microbes in your gut? All the hard work you put into eating lots of fiber and keeping those little guys fed vanishes when a round of antibiotics comes surging through your intestines. (I picture little kids bobbing innocently on floaties in the calm part of a pool when the operator suddenly turns on the waterslide and some aggro teenager comes barreling down the chute. Total wipeout!) The same thing happens when animals are given antibiotics. Like all bacteria, once the resistant ones are in the gut of an animal or a human, they can spread, either animal-to-people, such as by eating meat that's not thoroughly cooked, or people-to-people, through poor hygiene. They can also spread through the environment (such as when manure runoff from feedlots contaminates water sources that are then used to irrigate crops, which we end up eating).

It's not as if these bacteria stop at the border, so we're at risk when we import meat from other countries whose regulations about antibiotic use may be even more lax than ours. China, for instance, is far and away the heaviest user of antibiotics in food animal production—with a total tally that's forty times that of Norway. (Overall, European countries use less than half the global average per kilogram of meat produced.)

The scariest of all is what's called a superbug. Because it has developed resistance after repeated exposure to drugs that didn't manage to kill it, a superbug can deflect the powers of numerous different antibiotics, thereby wreaking havoc in your body.

WHAT YOU CAN DO

At the grocery store, use a plastic bag or other barrier to grab and wrap raw animal products—fish, shellfish, poultry, red meat—even though they are already wrapped in plastic. Keep them separate from other foods in your cart and refrigerator. Store them toward the bottom of your fridge so juices don't drip onto other foods, especially uncovered produce.

When cooking, handle raw meat with caution. Wash your hands with soap before and after touching it. (No need for antibacterial soap—the FDA concluded it's no more effective than regular soap.) To avoid cross-contamination, use a designated cutting board and knife for raw meat. Be sure to cook meat sufficiently, because even bacteria that can't be taken down by antibiotics can be thwarted by enough heat from your oven, slow cooker, or grill. Soon after cooking, store leftovers in the fridge.

Support better practices at the supermarket. Thanks to both consumer demand and policy pressure, the poultry industry especially has made huge strides to reduce its reliance on antibiotics. For example, Perdue and Tyson, two of the largest US producers, have eliminated antibiotics from their broiler chickens entirely. In part because cows and pigs take longer to raise than chickens and turkeys, progress in the beef and pork industry has been slower, but gradually things are moving in the right direction. To ensure responsible use of antibiotics by the producers behind the meat you buy, look for the following third-party certification labels:

* "Animal Welfare Approved"

* "American Grassfed"

* "Certified Humane Raised and Handled"

* "Global Animal Partnership (GAP) Certified" (except for chickens)

* "Certified Organic"

* Or any of the following three phrases: "Raised without antibiotics," "No antibiotics administered," and "No antibiotics ever." However, note that "antibiotic-free" is a misleading label whose meaning is unspecified. That's not the one to look for.

Support better farm practices at restaurants. Largely thanks to consumer demand, most of the top twenty-five chain restaurants have made the shift away from antibiotics for chicken. See "'Healthy' Fast Food" in Part 4 for a breakdown of how they stack up and how to help speed along the slackers, especially on the beef and swine fronts. If you don't see a mention on the menu, ask your server if the restaurant sources only animals raised without antibiotics.

Spending a little extra to help limit antibiotic use isn't so much about you personally not ingesting antibiotics in the moment as it is about curbing the excessive total use of antibiotics over the long run. Your individual action is essential to protecting the greater good.

34

PROCESSED MEAT AND CANCER

ot dogs and baseball. Bacon and weekends. Lunch boxes and ham sandwiches. American culture has a great many joyous associations with processed meats.

So it was tempting for many of us to look the other way when the World Health Organization released a whammy of a headline in 2015, stating that processed meat causes cancer. Colorectal cancer, specifically. This is a big deal. Rarely do scientists use the word *cause*. Normally you hear them cautiously, almost timidly, state a conclusion as, "Well, perhaps there's, at most, a 95 percent probability that Thing 1 *might*, given the weight of the evidence, have been *associated* with Thing 2—though more research is needed." When they say "cause," it means this is one scientific conclusion worth some serious attention.

The "processed meat" category includes hot dogs, ham, bacon, sausage, salami, corned beef, beef jerky, canned meat, and sauces made with those products, like a pork sausage ragù or bacon salad dressing. "Processing" in this context means meat that has been treated in order to preserve it over a long period of time or give it flavor—usually through smoking, salting, curing, or fermenting in some way. Most commonly, processed meats come from pork or beef, but the issue applies to those with a base of other red meats, poultry, meat by-products, or animal organs. There isn't the same level of consensus about whether smoked and cured fish products—think lox on your bagel—count as processed meats in terms of carrying the same cancer risk, but it makes sense to treat them

PROCESSED MEATS: CONSUME WITH CAUTION

According to the World Health Organization, eating processed meat causes cancer.

with similar caution since the American Institute for Cancer Research (AICR) puts them in the same boat. Americans tend to consume such a relatively small amount of smoked salmon and the like that the association isn't as clear in the research data. I'm afraid that, for now, this is one of those "more research is needed" moments. But the AICR also notes that preserving foods in general through salting (including pickled vegetables) increases the risk of stomach cancer, and one study of a specific type of cured fish—Cantonese-style salted fish—found an increased risk of nasopharyngeal cancer.

Even though eating poultry or fish instead of red meat might help protect against some cancers, and even though it's the red meats that pose additional concerns, opting for turkey bacon over pork bacon or chicken sausage over beef sausage or smoked whitefish over roast beef doesn't necessarily get you off the hook. The reason is that the root issue is the processing, though it's not yet understood which aspect of the processing causes the problems in the body. It could be the salting, the nitrates or nitrites that are added as preservatives, the smoking itself, or, of course, some combination. (Organic and nitrate-free meats usually use celery juice, a natural nitrate, but it's unclear whether the net effect is better.)

But be aware of the bigger picture: Aside from not smoking cigarettes, according to the AICR, maintaining a healthy weight is the most effective thing you can do to protect against cancer. So, although it's still wise to consume smoked and cured fish products in moderation, ultimately if those foods help you maintain a healthy weight (especially in place of other foods that would be less healthy), that's likely your stronger protection against not just colorectal but a range of cancers.

With its 2015 announcement, the WHO also proclaimed red meat as "probably carcinogenic," which means it has been tied to greater cancer risk. The "probably" part means researchers did not think the data was strong enough to say the connection was definitive, because other lifestyle variables could be at play. Red meat—i.e., meat from mammals, which in the United States are most commonly beef, pork, and lamb—was linked to not only colorectal cancer but pancreatic and prostate cancer. If the data grew to the point that the experts felt comfortable saying the effect was causal, the size of the risk would be that eating 100 grams of red meat per day—roughly a quarter-pound burger patty—would increase the chance of the cancers mentioned by 17 percent.

THE WHO ANNOUNCEMENT WAS PARTLY TAKEN OUT OF CONTEXT / SENSATIONALIZED IN THE MEDIA. THREE IMPORTANT CLARIFICATIONS:

* The effect appears when eating quite a bit of processed meat. Specifically, the researchers found that people who ate about six strips of bacon or a single hot dog's worth of

processed meat *every day* had an 18 percent higher chance of colorectal cancer.

* Context is key. That may as well become your default mantra whenever you absorb new information about what's healthy or not, or somewhere in between. In the processed meat case, an 18 percent *increased* risk means you go from the baseline of a 5 percent chance over the course of your entire life that you'll get colorectal cancer to about a 6 percent chance.

* The chance of getting cancer and dying because of eating processed meat is not the same as the chance of getting cancer and dying because of smoking. That both are in the Group 1 designation by the WHO's International Agency for Research on Cancer means they share the same strength of scientific evidence in terms of ties to cancer. That's a pretty wonky classification system for most of us regular consumers. It basically means there's a lot of scientific evidence for the connection to cancer in both cases. This particular finding came from an analysis of 800 studies by twenty-two experts representing ten different countries. But for perspective about the relative magnitude of this increased risk, the number of cancer deaths worldwide that can be attributed to eating lots of processed meat is about 34,000 per year. The number of cancer deaths from smoking tobacco is 1,000,000; from excess alcohol, 600,000; and from exposure to air pollution, 200,000.

Importantly, though, as discussed, there is still plenty of evidence that consuming high amounts of red and processed meat (when eaten instead of better protein sources like fish, poultry, and legumes) can lead to plenty of *other* diseases—from heart disease and stroke to type 2 diabetes—and increase one's overall chance of death. So, looking more holistically, the total number of annual deaths worldwide—not just those from cancer—that can be attributed to eating lots of processed meat is 644,000. That's according to the Harvard T. H. Chan School of Public Health's assessment of the Global Burden of Disease Project, which was based on data for the year 2013.

All in all, the World Cancer Research Fund recommends eating little (if any) processed meat and limiting red meat to about three portions per week. A portion is no more than 6 ounces cooked or 8 ounces raw—for a *maximum* of 18 ounces cooked, or 24 ounces raw, of red meat per week.

To recap: There are heaps of data that something about processed meats messes with our cell functioning and raises our risk of colorectal cancer. However, you don't have to give them up entirely.

SENSIBLE SOLUTIONS FOR PROCESSED MEAT CONSUMPTION

* Try to get deli meats sliced fresh from the butcher counter. That way you'll avoid or at least reduce the amount of nitrates added for preservation. Whole roasted chickens at the grocery store are considered fresh, too, not processed.

* Though more research is needed, you'd be wise to choose verifiably healthy cooking methods for your fish intake (like baking), and treat lox and the like as special treats.

* Don't eat bacon every day for breakfast, or bologna sandwiches every day for lunch. Your frequent habits make a *much* bigger difference for your long-term health than what you eat on special occasions. Which means . . .

* Yes, every now and then at a baseball game, go ahead and enjoy that hot dog.

35

YOUR DIET AND CANCER

For each of us, the chance of developing one or more types of cancer throughout the span of our lifetime depends on a complicated cocktail of factors. Genes play a role, but for some cancers, genes are not nearly as influential as lifestyle and environmental factors. The following lifestyle choices deliver the biggest bang for your buck, probability-wise:

* Don't smoke.

* Maintain a healthy weight. Aside from not smoking, this is the single most helpful thing you can do to minimize your risk of getting cancer. It's protective for twelve different types of cancer. To get there, sustain the habits that together do a body good—exercise and eat well. Some of this is up to you and your willpower, yet the feasibility of these habits is also heavily influenced by our environments, meaning the extent to which we each have access to healthy and affordable food choices, clean air, safe outdoor space, and so on. Good news: These lifestyle factors are the same ones that keep down your risk for heart disease and diabetes. Three birds, one stone.

* Use smart sun protection, from wearing sunglasses and hats to applying sunscreen and seeking shade. Though non-melanoma skin cancers—basal and squamous cell carcinomas—are not tracked in cancer registries in the same way most cancers are, together they make skin cancer considered the most common type of cancer in the United States.

The reason I'm reminding you about the importance of sunscreen and exercise in a food book is to provide some additional context for the previous discussion on processed and red meats and for the relative impact that overall food choices have on your lifetime cancer risk. As for cancer-protective foods, there's a great resource from the American Institute for Cancer Research and the World Cancer Research Fund called the Interactive Cancer Risk Matrix (you can find it at *wcrf.org*). It plots various diet, nutrition, and physical activity factors with how much they lower or raise cancer risk. What jumps out from that map—aside from the reinforcement around both red and processed meat—are a few key findings related to what and how we eat:

* Breastfeeding and having been breastfed as a baby are hugely beneficial. It lowers breast cancer risk for lactating mothers and decreases cancer risk for children, mainly because of the protective effects against being overweight or obese.

* Fiber is your friend! See "Fermented Foods and Fiber" in Part 1 for a refresher. Specifically, eat plenty of whole grains, legumes, fruits, and vegetables.

* Too much alcohol, as well as fast food and the overall Western diet, are hugely detrimental.

All in all, cancer risk is a complex probability potpourri. Unfortunately, an estimated 38 percent of Americans will develop cancer at some point in their lifetimes. However, thanks to advances in anti-cancer therapeutics, the overall US death rate caused by cancer has declined substantially since the 1990s—as have the death rates for the four most commonly diagnosed types of cancer (excluding those basal cell and squamous cell skin cancers), which are breast, colorectal, lung, and prostate. Ultimately, if you can sustain habits that are generally good for health and body weight—eat a flexitarian diet consisting of mostly whole foods, avoid tobacco, keep alcohol in moderation, and move your body each day—you will at the same time reduce your total lifetime odds of getting cancer.

 Take charge! To get a feel for your individual risk for not only twelve cancers but six common chronic diseases—and gain ideas for preventing them— I highly recommend spending some time with the interactive online resource *yourdiseaserisk.org*. Provided by the Siteman Cancer Center at Washington University in St. Louis, the Your Disease Risk™ tool is rigorously designed yet extremely user-friendly.

36

8 TRICKS TO LOWER
THE CANCER RISK OF GRILLING

I include this essay at the risk of never being invited to another summer barbecue again. No one wants me and my party-pooping news lurking around the Weber while they're trying to enjoy this sacred summer pastime. But before you jump to "ignorance is bliss," the bright side is that there are easy ways to lower the health concerns posed by grilling. And they won't feel like much of a sacrifice.

When you grill, two compounds are created: polycyclic aromatic hydrocarbons (PAHs) and heterocyclic amines (HCAs). The former happens from the smoke, and the latter happens from a reaction that takes place only in meat.

These compounds don't *cause* cancer, per se. As you'll recall, *cause* is a word they take very seriously in the cancer research world, saving it for those times when the evidence is overwhelmingly clear. However, in lab studies, these compounds have been found to alter DNA in a way that *could* lead to cancer. For this reason, researchers and public health experts urge diners to avoid them as best we can. Each year, in fact, the American Institute for Cancer Research (AICR) publishes a guide to "cancer-safe grilling."

PAHs come from the combustion of organic matter—most often fat dripping from cooking meat and falling between grill grates. Those potentially carcinogenic hydrocarbons get swept up in the smoke and coat the meat. HCAs are easier to identify. They're the black char that's the trademark of the grilling experience. They are formed when any type of muscle meat—red meat (usually beef, pork, and lamb), poultry (usually chicken, duck, and turkey), or fish—comes in contact with high temperatures. Amino acids react with creatine, a substance within the meat.

As we've discussed, when it comes to dialing up or down your risk of cancer or really any health issue, the dose makes the poison. If you're grilling once or twice a year, I say don't sweat it. But it's worth some caution if, like me, you enjoy grilling more regularly (more like once or twice a week throughout the summer). It's best to steer clear of both of these substances to the extent possible.

HERE ARE EIGHT WAYS TO ENJOY THE FUN AND FLAVOR OF GRILLING WHILE KEEPING YOUR CANCER RISK TO A MINIMUM.

1   THINK OUTSIDE THE BURGER. See the previous two essays for a refresher on why the choices you make about *what* to eat (and therefore to grill) are arguably the most important in terms of cancer risk. **Bottom line:** Enjoy a burger or brat every now and then if you like, absolutely, but for more frequent barbecuing, opt for plant-based foods as much as possible, along with fish, seafood, and poultry, rather than making red meat and processed meat your defaults.

2   MARINATE FIRST. Studies have suggested that marinating meat or fish for at least thirty minutes before grilling can reduce the formation of HCAs. That's doubly great news since it also makes those foods taste better. Researchers aren't exactly sure why marinating helps, but one possibility is a kind of shield effect: It coats the outside of the meat, essentially creating a barrier between it and the heat.

3   MAKE PRODUCE THE STAR. Many fruits and vegetables actually help protect you from cancer, plus they don't form HCAs when grilled. If those don't excite you as a whole meal,

though, try the classic kabob approach—for example, alternating cubed chicken with sliced bell peppers, zucchini, and onions, or a fruit twist such as peaches or pineapple.

4   BE MINDFUL OF THE SMOKE ITSELF. We all know it's bad to inhale cigarette smoke, but the same goes for smoke from a grill. Try not to breathe in too much, especially if you're the grillmaster or nice enough to keep the grillmaster company.

5   AVOID CHAR. Take this piece of advice in particular with a substantial dose of radical practicality: No one is asking you to scrape the grill marks off your chicken breast one by one. But sometimes that black, crispy char is easy to remove before eating or to simply avoid—picture the bony edges of ribs or steak. You're best off trimming it or not biting into it since the crust is more likely to contain more of these compounds. A related tip from the National Cancer Institute is to flip often: If you regularly turn the meat over while cooking it on the grill, you can reduce the amount of HCAs that are formed. And to get rid of the char from last weekend's party, clean your grill grates each time.

6   LEVERAGE HERBS AND SPICES. Research also suggests that cooking your meat with ingredients high in antioxidants—such as certain herbs, spices, teas, and chile peppers—can mitigate the amount of potentially carcinogenic compounds that get formed.

7 CUT TIME ON THE GRILL. The AICR recommends partially pre-cooking your meat (such as by baking or in the microwave) to minimize the length of time it is exposed to the flame. The explanation is that the longer the chemical reaction takes place, the thicker the charred crust and the higher the concentration of HCAs. The institute also suggests cutting meat into smaller pieces so it will cook faster. (Again: kabobs.) For its part, the Harvard T. H. Chan School of Public Health offers a guide to healthy picnics, which suggests grilling in foil to speed up cooking time. They note that you'll also expose the food to less smoke that way.

8 REDUCE FUEL FOR THE FIRE, SO TO SPEAK. To minimize your exposure to PAHs, experts recommend selecting leaner cuts of meat or trimming any visible fat. Not piercing your meats while they're on the grill is suggested for the same reason, which is to lower the amount of fats or juices that drip down through the grates and come back up in the smoke.

37

STICKERS TO KNOW

What do all those little symbols and buzzwords mean on the side or bottom corner of a package? Beyond health, the third-party certification labels selected below are among the most meaningful signifiers of superior social, animal welfare, or environmental considerations. Some are regulated by federal agencies, and others are provided by advocacy groups or NGOs. They apply to the wide range of stuff that comes from animals. Align your values with these labels' assurances to decide where best to spend your extra grocery dollars.

CERTIFIED ORGANIC OR USDA ORGANIC

What it means: The standards prohibit a range of practices and substances, but it boils down to

* no synthetic pesticides,

* no growth hormones, and

* no antibiotics.

On a label for a processed food product, USDA organic certification means that 95 percent or more of the ingredients in the product were certified organic.

What it doesn't mean: That the product itself is nutritious. It also does not guarantee ambitious animal welfare standards, so if those are important to you, look for a label other than organic certification.

Who's behind it: US Department of Agriculture (USDA)

Why it's legit: It has among the most rigorous and comprehensive standards as far as how a food is grown or raised. In short, these standards can support ecosystems and farmworkers' health (though not necessarily their wages) because the farming practices are less intensive than conventional methods.

ANIMAL WELFARE APPROVED

What it means: Animals were raised on family farms and free to "engage in their natural behaviors." Applied to those raised for meat, dairy, or eggs, this label reflects one of the few times when reality actually aligns with the image most consumers have in their minds of what humane animal husbandry ought to look like: living outside, on pasture. A full list of humane practices encapsulated in this label by species can be found at *greenerchoices.org*.

What it doesn't mean: That other environmentally sustainable farming practices were necessarily used, though they are encouraged. That said, if pesticides and herbicides were used, animals with this label would be kept off the treated areas for at least three weeks.

Who's behind it: A Greener World

Why it's legit: This is the top-rated animal welfare certification on the market, according to Consumer Reports.

CERTIFIED HUMANE RAISED AND HANDLED

What it means: Chickens and pigs get comfy bedding and clean litter, there are no small cages prohibiting free movement, and, most concerning, physical alterations (like docking pig tails) are prohibited, whereas others—like trimming the beaks of laying hens—are allowed. The latter is done so the hens don't peck each other to death and is considered less invasive and more humane than debeaking. Of course, this wouldn't be necessary if flocks were given enough space to move around freely. For the most part, slaughter standards of animals are higher than industry norms.

What it doesn't mean: Access to the outdoors and fresh air for these animals, which of course most of us would expect from a "Certified Humane" label.

Who's behind it: Humane Farm Animal Care

Why it's legit: This is Consumer Reports' second-highest-rated animal welfare certification, though it's considered "meaningful" only for animal welfare, rather than the gold standard of "highly meaningful" bestowed to "Animal Welfare Approved." Representatives from the Humane Society of the United States and the NGO Farm Forward also both cite this as a top animal welfare label.

GLOBAL ANIMAL PARTNERSHIP (GAP) CERTIFIED

What it means: It represents several standards for animal welfare, tailored to specific species, in a five-step program. Step 1: no cages, crates, or crowding; Step 2: enriched environment; Step 3: enhanced outdoor access; Step 4: pasture-centered; Step 5: animal-centered and no physical alterations; Step 5+: animal-centered and their entire life is spent on the same farm (except for chickens, which may be transferred right before slaughter). It also means no growth hormones, animal by-products in any species' feed, or antibiotics (except for chickens). This is the highest rating available.

What it doesn't mean: To date, it applies only to meat and eggs, so it does not apply to the animal care behind dairy products.

Who's behind it: Global Animal Partnership

Why it's legit: Participating farms get audited every fifteen months and are encouraged to move up the ladder over time. Whole Foods Market, a clear retail leader with respect to consumers' right to transparency about what they're buying, helped launch the program back in 2008.

NO ANTIBIOTICS

What it means: This is a category of terms, not a specific label, so the point here is simply to persuade you to allocate your animal-product grocery dollars to support any verified indication of lower uses of antibiotics that are medically important to humans. Guess what? All four of the labels I just listed already check this box, as does American Grassfed, the next one down. In the absence of a third-party logo certification, other phrases that are legit include "Raised without antibiotics," "No antibiotics administered," and "No antibiotics ever." Note that "Antibiotic-free" is a misleading label whose meaning is unspecified.

What it doesn't mean: That other comprehensive practices—whether for animal welfare, farmworker health, or environmental sustainability—were involved. For those, turn to certified organic and the other more specific third-party assurances.

Who's behind it: Varies, but usually the producer

Why it's legit: It's critically important for public health that producers reduce the use of antibiotics in the food supply. Only then can we ensure that the ones used in human medicine remain effective.

AMERICAN GRASSFED

What it means: The cow—or goat, lamb, or bison—really ate only grass or forage (or hay, which is dried grass, in winter). The exception is when they (rightfully) had milk from their mother before they were weaned. It also means animals were raised only on pasture, so they didn't experience cruel confinement in feedlots, they didn't receive antibiotics or growth hormones, and they were born and raised on American family farms.

What it doesn't mean: That other rigorous humane practices were involved once they left the farm (such as en route to slaughter), though electric prods are generally prohibited.

Who's behind it: American Grassfed Association

Why it's legit: All of the cattle that get turned into beef eat some grass during their lives, but how much is the big question, because ruminant animals are simply not designed to eat grain. Consumer Reports considers "American Grassfed" one of the most meaningful ways of knowing these animals were raised on a diet that's good for them. As discussed earlier, healthy animals are healthy for humans and the planet, too.

PCO CERTIFIED 100% GRASSFED

What it means: The cow really ate only grass or forage (or hay in winter). This label applies to beef and dairy products specifically.

What it doesn't mean: Again, that rigorous humane animal welfare practices were involved, though the standards of organic are strictly enforced.

Who's behind it: Pennsylvania Certified Organic organization

Why it's legit: Healthy diets of dairy cows yield many benefits similar to those of beef cattle, and the FDA doesn't regulate the definition of *grass-fed* for dairy products, so this label is particularly helpful.

SEAFOOD WATCH "BEST CHOICE," "GOOD ALTERNATIVE," AND "AVOID" LABELS

What it means: You won't find the labels on fish products themselves, but free, downloadable guides are available for all fifty states, as is a mobile phone app so you can easily reference which types of fish and seafood are considered best, worst, and in between. Seafood Watch uses a three-part rating scheme: "Best" (labeled green) means the fish are caught or farmed using methods that are minimally damaging to marine life and environments. They exist in

abundant supply. "Good" (labeled yellow) means they're fine for you to buy, but some issues have been identified with how they are caught or farmed. "Avoid" (labeled red) means they're caught or farmed in harmful ways and/or that they are overfished. The criteria behind these categories are based on the optimal locations of origin, species type, and aquaculture methods or fishing equipment.

What it doesn't mean: That fair prices were necessarily given to the fishermen or fisherwomen, or that those individuals caught the fish under humane work conditions. For those issues, Seafood Watch developed the separate Seafood Slavery Risk Tool.

Who's behind it: Monterey Bay Aquarium

Why it's legit: By far the most comprehensive, trusted, and widely recognized certifier of sustainable seafood on the market, it is used by both retailers and restaurants to ensure fish and shellfish choices that do not deplete certain species or degrade oceans or waterways.

MARINE STEWARDSHIP COUNCIL'S BLUE FISH LABEL

What it means: It provides third-party assurance that *wild-caught* fish and seafood products have been certified as sustainable,

which is especially useful if you're not sure where an item stands in Seafood Watch's book. You can find it at the fish counter and on fish products, supplements (like fish oil), and even pet food.

What it doesn't mean: That the same standards apply to farmed fish and seafood. For those, refer to Seafood Watch, again, or to the Aquaculture Stewardship Council's certification scheme.

Who's behind it: Marine Stewardship Council, a UK-based organization that developed the first certification for wild, sustainable seafood

Why it's legit: To be certified, fisheries must meet twenty-eight carefully audited criteria across three key principles that make up their definition of *sustainable*: fish caught from stocks whose populations are thriving, in ways that minimally impact the surrounding environment, and from regions where fishery management is up to snuff. No wonder Monterey Bay Aquarium endorses them, since their standards are clearly aligned.

AQUACULTURE STEWARDSHIP COUNCIL CERTIFICATION

What it means: It provides third-party assurance that *farmed* fish and seafood products have been certified as environmentally sustainable  and socially responsible, which is especially useful if you're not sure where an item stands in Seafood Watch's book. Their strict standards minimize the impact of fish farming on water quality and surrounding habitats and marine life, require responsible disease management, and enforce fair wages and good working conditions for workers in the industry, including prohibiting both child labor and forced labor.

What it doesn't mean: That the same standards apply to wild-caught fish and seafood. For those, refer to Seafood Watch or the Marine Stewardship Council's blue fish label.

Who's behind it: Aquaculture Stewardship Council

Why it's legit: Their framework is about as rigorous as you can find for food farmed from the sea.

REFRESHER ON THE MEANINGS OF EGG LABELS
MEANINGFUL

"Animal Welfare Approved." Considered the top animal welfare label on the market by Consumer Reports, this label represents producers who have gone well beyond cage-free or free-range or ensuring appropriate feed. It means animals are given the freedom to engage in their natural behaviors. For egg-laying hens, you can imagine chickens allowed to walk around, peck for bugs, nest, and so on.

"Certified Humane Raised and Handled." This certification ensures that specific standards have been met for one of the three levels related to eggs—cage-free, free-range, or pasture-raised. If you see this label, you'll also see one of those three designations.

"Global Animal Partnership (GAP) Certified." This is a five-step program tailored to specific species and includes egg-laying hens. Look for these different steps, which have different label colors: Step 1: no cages, crates, or crowding; Step 2: enriched environments; Step 3: enhanced outdoor access; Step 4: pasture-centered; Step 5: animal-centered and no physical alterations; Step 5+: animal-centered and their entire lives are spent on the same farm (except for chickens, which may be transferred right before slaughter). It also means no growth hormones, animal by-products in any species' feed, or antibiotics (except for chickens). This is the highest rating available.

"No Antibiotics." This means egg producers did not add antibiotics to the feed or water of the egg-laying chickens.

"Certified Organic." Carefully regulated by the USDA, organic certification sets specific requirements for what egg-laying hens are fed—the food must be vegetarian and free from pesticides or antibiotics—and how the land they're raised on is treated. So, it's a strong one from environmental and public health standpoints. Where it's not so strong is animal welfare. For assurance of access to the outdoors or more extensive lifestyle enhancements for the birds, look for the aforementioned animal welfare labels or the more rigorous versions of "pasture-raised" or "free-range," as described below.

SOMEWHERE IN BETWEEN

"Cage-Free." Hens are likely still raised in very confined quarters squished up against each other, and they may or may not be let outdoors. But at least they're not in tiny cages, and in theory they are free to move around and do their usual chicken thing. Cage-free means a heck of a lot more when buying eggs—whose hens are indeed most commonly confined to cruelly small cages—than it does when buying chicken, because broilers aren't usually raised in cages to begin with.

"Free-Range" or **"Free-Roaming."** This one is often interchangeable with "cage-free," except its extra selling point is outdoor access. Again, it's best if it's attached to a third-party verification for animal welfare standards.

"Pasture-Raised." A fairly good indicator, the term means birds were mostly raised outside and let loose to roam and forage for food. Consider it a notch above free-range and cage-free. That said, it's not enforced by the USDA, so the exact meaning is rather hazy. Your best bet is to trust this claim when it is paired with one of the legit animal welfare labels like "Certified Humane Raised and Handled."

"Vegetarian-Fed." This is fairly straightforward, but the reason it's noteworthy is that a lot of agribusiness involves feeding food animals parts of other animals. Although this issue isn't as relevant in the egg industry as it is in meat and poultry, it can be a reassurance for some shoppers, and especially vegetarian shoppers.

"Omega-3s." This label means the hens' feed included one of the main sources of omega-3 fatty acids—most commonly fish oil, flaxseeds, or flaxseed oil. Although you can indeed add to your daily omega-3 tally this way, the challenge is knowing which type of omega-3 and how much you're getting, since the conversion to human nutrients is unclear on the packaging and not required on the label. These eggs are probably perfectly fine to eat but can sometimes be a waste of the extra money. You might focus your omega-hunting attentions elsewhere in your diet, such as by eating the fish or flaxseed directly.

TOP 5 TAKEAWAYS

1 Transparency and traceability are the names of the game. Ask questions. It's your right to know what's in your food and how it got to you.

2 Rely on third-party certifications to know how food animals are raised—from sustainable fisheries management to responsible livestock production. Auditors are the referees of the transparency and traceability game.

3 Whenever you eat an animal or animal product, you're also eating whatever that creature ate—in other words, you are what you eat *eats*. So, in addition to animal welfare, be cognizant of animal diets. Ultimately, their food is your food.

4 In the face of seedy practices—treating animals and workers inhumanely, fishing illegally, adulterating premium products—don't get mad, get even. Vote with your grocery basket.

5 If you don't feel compelled to go full vegan or vegetarian, you don't have to apologize. So long as you're eating a variety of healthy foods—and not too much from animals— you can still be a conscious eater by making responsible choices about those foods.

PART 3

STUFF THAT COMES FROM FACTORIES

With almost every inch of food packaging covered in superlatives shouting the product's attributes, inspecting an item in the grocery store can feel like being in a noisy, one-sided conversation. This section will empower you to navigate that noise. On the whole, the healthiest foods are, well, whole. They don't need marketing claims in the first place. Reducing the amount of packaging in our foodscape—especially single-use plastics—would also go a long way toward improving your health and the planet's health. But there are plenty of minimally or moderately processed foods that are quite virtuous in all three respects of the *Conscious Eater Checklist*.

As a general rule, the idea of "clean labels"—those with a small number of ingredients with simple, intuitive-sounding names—definitely has some merit. Ingredients with fewer syllables. Ingredients your grandmother would recognize as food. To most consumers, *clean* means *natural*. But since that remains a murkily defined term, *clean* has instead come to mean *familiar*. The clean-label movement has brought about a reckoning with the question of what ingredients and steps in a "process" are truly necessary to make a given food company's processed food product work. Bright colors, shelf life, consistent texture and flavor—these are traits we've come to expect from the products lining our shelves. They've been the backbone of that industry for decades. But packaged-food giants have reformulated with a vengeance to stay relevant. More progressive companies are even expanding their meanings of *clean* to include ethical sourcing and sustainability standards.

With many land mines between you and the stuff that comes from factories, this section will help you determine which packaged foods are worth bringing home—or back to your desk, or to your kid's playdate—with clear eyes and confidence.

38

PROCESSED FOODS: NOT ALL BAD

Not all "processed foods" are unhealthy. They often get a bad rap because they get grouped together with *ultra-processed* foods, which tend to be detrimental health-wise, or nutritionally empty at best. But they include any food that has been altered in some way from its original state, through means like drying, canning, freezing, milling, and pasteurizing. And plenty of items that have been "processed" to some degree can, without question, be considered beneficial to health. Olive oil; frozen vegetables; chopped fruit; breads, pastas, and crackers that are 100 percent whole-grain; canned tomatoes, chickpeas, beans, sardines, tuna, salmon, and other fish (when they don't have too much sodium); fermented foods like yogurt and kimchi; and all the nut butters are processed foods that are truly good for you. Alcoholic drinks of all sorts can be considered processed foods as well, and surely they're one of our species' greatest innovations.

However, we know that the healthiest foods tend to be whole foods. They don't require us to decode labels and claims because they don't have any. Fresh fruits and vegetables aren't swathed in signage. They don't shout their vitamin profile or their high fiber content. They don't tout their cancer-fighting properties or their low calorie count. For better or worse, whole foods rely on knowledge we bring into the store rather than on information we absorb upon arrival: a personal history of whether we liked the taste, felt good after eating the foods, or enjoyed them paired with certain other foods; awareness of whether they're good for our health, good for others, and good for the environment; and knowledge of when they're ripe, when they're in season, and what to do with them once they land on the kitchen counter.

But almost everything else in the store is not food so much as what author Michael Pollan calls "edible foodlike substances." Or a new favorite term of mine, from author Kristin Lawless, it's stuff "formerly known as food." These products rely on their packaging to speak to us as consumers. Price plays a key role in our decisions, of course, but so does language.

Processed foods do unfortunately tend to come in cartons or cans or bags or boxes, but most of them are increasingly available to buy in bulk or on tap (such as oats and beer) or to make through DIY kits or online guides (such as pasta and yogurt). When a food category *can* be replicated at home, it's a telling sign that it's lower on the processing spectrum, given that most of us don't have hydrolyzed soy protein lying around our spice cabinets or seasoning drums hanging out in the garage.

It's not as if all chemicals or additives are automatically unhealthy. It's just that in the regulatory environment of the US food supply, it's a tall order to remember which ones are fine and which ones to steer clear of. Beyond the ingredients list, the challenge is discerning those products that truly are what you're looking for from those that are misleading.

Although it's a helpful general rule, that a product has only a short list of simple ingredients doesn't automatically make it good for you. Think of butter, for example. On the stick, it might list just one ingredient (for example, "sweet cream"), but that doesn't mean it's healthy. A peanut butter label might tout "just four ingredients," when really it should have just one: peanuts. Maybe a dash of salt. But what are the rest of those ingredients doing in there? Nutella has ingredients I mostly recognize (sugar, hazelnuts, cocoa), but it also has 21 grams of sugar per serving (out of a suggested daily limit of 25–36 grams total) and palm oil as the second ingredient, so it's not exactly healthy. Though at least it uses exclusively certified sustainable palm oil, so you know it was sourced in a responsible way.

In addition, there's a lot of hooey peddled along with the sometimes cultlike clean-eating evangelism. So, beware the trap of oversimplification and overdoing any one thing. There's a saying in public health that the dose makes the poison. In other words, clichés like "everything in moderation" and "variety is the spice of life" have real scientific reasoning behind them. Foods aren't "good" or "bad" in isolation; how much you eat of them—at one time, and how often—makes all the difference in how they affect your body. This applies both positively and negatively, as when consumers suffer from orthorexia: an unhealthy obsession with eating clean. Like anorexia and obsessive-compulsive disorder, it's a fixation centered on control. Refusing to eat foods that one does not consider pure can actually have quite unfortunate consequences, from damaged social ties and compromised mental health to malnourishment. (Check out Bee Wilson's article in *The Guardian* on why we fell for clean eating.)

The bottom line is yes, aim to eat mostly whole foods, especially plant-based foods, but don't feel guilty for eating *some* processed foods. Because *healthy* is more nuanced than simply *processed* = *unhealthy*.

39

HOLDING WATER

I t's funny how many of the same people who go to great lengths to tote their reusable water bottles to meetings or drink their coffees from reusable thermos mugs will churn through three cans of LaCroix in a day. I know because I've been one of these people!

When possible, buy in bulk and store in your own containers. This extends well beyond food products to cleaning products, beauty products, and pretty much anything you can put in your shopping cart (whether that cart be physical or digital). That's because disposable and single-serving containers have a high environmental footprint. Someone has to mine or collect the raw packaging material, which often disrupts surrounding habitat. Then someone has to transport and process the packaging material to factories, which involves transportation fuel and energy at the processing plant. Then there's the environmental cost of recycling and turning the source material into other products. Whether it's an aluminum can, plastic jug, glass bottle, or cardboard box, you're better off with the alternative: a reusable container from home. Inconvenient? Sometimes, but if you can develop the habit (as millions of us have already been trained to do with reusable grocery bags), there's financial reward. What's good for the planet can be good for your pocket.

If it's fizzy water you're after, consider a home bubble maker. SodaStream is a popular choice, and the infinitely reusable glass carafe makes it an even better investment, since other models' large plastic bottles can degrade over time. There are other options as well, both more and less expensive. Some quick napkin arithmetic suggests that after the up-front investment of at most $200, and with an exchange rate of $15 for your 60-liter carbonation cylinder, you're looking at 25 cents per liter—tops. That's one-fourth the price of an average liter of grocery store seltzer, meaning a savings of at least 75 cents a pop.

If it's plain water we're talking about, consider the feel-good reward of your individual action: Each time you hydrate with a glass of water versus a plastic bottle of water, you're conserving 2,400 calories of energy involved in producing that bottle. That's a whole day's worth of food for someone.

But if you have to choose a drink in a single-serving container of some kind—plastic bottle, aluminum can, or glass bottle—choose glass. It does the least damage to the planet. Ditto damage to you and others. Here's how the rest stack up.

In the most holistic environmental sense, plastic is by far the worst container option. (OK, Styrofoam is actually the worst, but it's so bad that it shouldn't even be under consideration.) It takes a lot of water to make a plastic bottle, and a lot of oil, and because it takes so many years for the bottle to degrade, it leaches toxic chemicals into the environment if the bottle winds up in a landfill somewhere (usually in low-income neighborhoods, already burdened with higher rates of chronic illnesses). It likely never gets recycled, especially in the United States, where we recycle a mere 9 percent of all plastic waste. Incinerators can pollute the air of the communities where plastic gets sent to be recycled. (To learn how plastic also wreaks havoc on *aquatic* communities, see "#StopSucking" on page 167.)

Cans are better, but not by much. The raw material behind your average can is bauxite ore, which requires a lot of energy to refine and has been found to leak toxic and ugly red mud residues, which can contaminate surrounding water sources. Dams built for hydroelectric power to process the aluminum can disrupt the biodiversity of the area and displace local communities. Although drinking from aluminum cans is generally considered quite safe, it's the BPA plastic lining of many canned products that is raising some concerns. BPA, an industrial chemical officially called bisphenol A, is used as a barrier for acidic foods—like tomatoes, soda, and beer, to name a few—where the liquid could react with the aluminum.

Aluminum is the most commonly recycled material of all, so props on that front, but glass still wins because of how it's made (melting silica sand, soda ash, and limestone, which are more easily available than environmentally destructive bauxite) and the fact that, of the three, it has the lowest total carbon footprint. Admittedly, that's based on a life-cycle assessment done by a glass manufacturer, but nonetheless, *Slate* has reported that it takes about twice the energy to make an aluminum can as it does an equivalent glass bottle. For the most complete picture of their respective environmental footprints, consider too whether the producer used any recycled materials. Although glass is less likely to be recycled in the formal sense, anecdotally it's more likely than aluminum to get reused (rolling pin, art project, place to store stewed tomatoes). And if we heed the motto of waste management—"Reduce, Reuse, Recycle"—we know that reusing is more environmentally responsible than recycling. Worth considering before you crush another can of sparkling water.

40

#STOPSUCKING

Our decades-long relationship with single-use plastics—straws, lids, bags, take-out containers, bottles, stirrers, single-serving snack packs—now seems rather abusive. Like a one-night stand, we get our quick fix, then kick the poor thing to the curb, paying its later whereabouts little mind. So, it's time for a breakup. If, like me, you've ever made a pros and cons list to drum up the courage to call it off with someone you know isn't right for you (sure, that high school boyfriend was cute and smart, but rude to my friends and way too clingy . . .), now seems like a good time to practice the old two-column tally.

PROS FOR USING SINGLE-USE PLASTICS:

Convenience. Ziplock sandwich bags sure are handy during the morning rush out the door, as are disposable stirrers when you don't have a spoon for the milk in your coffee, as are plastic take-out containers when you've got screaming kids in the backseat and need dinner to-go.

Portion control. For items like yogurt, bottled beverages, trail mix, chips, or other snacks, single-serving containers or packs help us consume only a healthy amount in one sitting.

Low impact on your budget. A whole crate of forty bottled waters costs a mere $4. Straws come free with your smoothie. And so on.

Light weight. Glass is a heavier vessel for any food or drink you're carting around in your backpack or purse.

Durability. Plastic containers bend and stretch and don't break if you drop them.

CONS AGAINST USING SINGLE-USE PLASTICS:

Plastic pollution is one of the most serious threats to the health of our oceans. About 18 billion pounds of plastic enter the ocean from coastal communities. One estimate suggests that by 2050 the ocean will house proportionally more plastic than fish. (!) Tragic scenes abound, from turtles choking on straws to whales' bellies so full of plastic, they starve because they can't fit in enough food. *National Geographic* has called the ocean "Earth's last sink." Bottles and bags are culprits, but straws are especially problematic because they are so small and lightweight, they often fall through the cracks of recycling sorters, don't get put in the recycling bin, or aren't accepted by recyclers in the first place. But straws are just the poster plastic for a much larger wake-up call about the need for sustainable packaging. And less packaging, period.

Microplastics. The enormous accumulation of all these little plastic particles in marine life could be making its way into our bodies when we eat the critters. Microplastics, as they're called, have shown up in more than 100 aquatic species, more than half of which are common human fare. These tiny plastic particles are degraded pieces of larger plastic debris. The science is still emerging, and so far it's not reason to stop eating shellfish and fish—the plastics don't yet appear to make their way into tissue, instead staying in their guts. Plus, it's hard to discern cause and effect, given the sadly plastic-filled world we inhabit on land as it is, from clothing to cosmetics. But because one of the themes of this book is that not only are you what you eat, but you are what you eat *eats* too, it's fair to say that if you don't want plastic in *your* body, you probably don't want plastic in your food's body either.

Consuming too much. The faster we ingest a large volume of sugar, the worse the effects on our blood sugar levels. So even though we can't blame plastic entirely, the fact that most straws are made out of plastic implicates the material as aiding and abetting some nasty effects on our waistlines and bloodstream: They can make slurping something super sugary—a Big Gulp of soda, a desserty Frappuccino—spike our blood sugar in ways that are no good from an insulin perspective, especially for anyone with diabetes or prediabetes.

BPA. Maybe you don't live near the ocean, aren't bothered by microparticles, or lack the bandwidth to reorganize your hectic week's worth of household responsibilities that are made eminently easier thanks to countless disposable plastics. Here are some more immediate reasons to care: Cancer. Childhood brain development. Hormone irregularity. High blood pressure. All have been associated with the chemical found not only lining many canned goods but in many single-use plastics like bottled water: BPA. (Weirdly, the chemical also lines most store register receipts.) More research is needed across the board, and the FDA says BPA is safe at the levels currently found in foods, but numerous academic researchers have been sounding alarm bells. Unfortunately, most of the BPA alternatives (BPS or BPF, commonly) appear to pose similar negative health risks. This means you should be cautious with even those plastic products labeled BPA-free. For texture similar to plastic for items like utensils, plates, cups, bowls, pouches, and bottles or bottle tops, especially for kids and baby products, look for silicone substitutes. In lieu of ziplock bags, dishwasher-safe cloth substitutes work great.

Phthalates. This is a word people inject into the argument right about now that never looks right on paper but is important to recognize and easier to say. (It's THAL-lates, if that helps.) Phthalates are endocrine disruptors, which means they interfere with the normal functioning of hormones in the body. They can make plastics like some food wraps and packaging soft, and the concern is that they may leach into foods themselves. Phthalates are found in such a dizzying number of consumer products—they're almost impossible to avoid completely. But at high levels they have been linked to compromised sperm quality, hormone function, and reproductive development among men, and to preterm birth and early-onset puberty among women.

Culturally, Americans are far more guilt-free about using disposable consumer goods than people in many other countries. Americans still use an average of nearly a plastic bag a day, for example, whereas people living in Denmark use four *a year*.

Bottom line: Whatever you care most about—oceans of plastic or oceans of health reasons—it's time to part ways.

41

10 WAYS TO PART WAYS WITH PLASTIC

A s with most lifestyle changes, calling it quits on one thing you do/eat/use means finding a suitable replacement thing to do/eat/use instead. *Here are ten ways to break up with plastic, complete with suitable rebound candidates.*

1   **MAKE GLASS YOUR GO-TO.** For storing, transporting, drinking, and eating, choose **glass** when possible. Stainless steel and silicone are also good choices.

2   **NEVER HEAT PLASTIC.** Many meals come in plastic containers —soup, frozen dinners, take-out food, leftovers from a restaurant, preportioned prepared foods from the grocery deli counter. When possible, keep plastic containers to a minimum—bring your own containers to your favorite restaurant for takeout or to use for any leftovers—but if you do end up with a plastic container, do not heat your food in it. Warmer temperatures leach plastic chemicals into your food and drink. Instead, pour them into a different vessel before warming them up— heat-safe glass, porcelain, or ceramic containers to microwave or to heat on the stovetop or in the oven. For the same reason, don't put most plastic containers in the dishwasher.

3 SKIP SINGLE-USE BEVERAGE BOTTLES. In the United States alone, as reported by *National Geographic*, each of us has been buying an average of 346 plastic drink bottles a year—nearly one a day. At your desk or your home, just use a plain old glass or mug. Away from home, bring a refillable stainless steel or glass water bottle. Do I expect us all to go cold turkey overnight? Of course not. If you're on an airplane, dehydrated, without a reusable container, by all means, drink some bottled water. Ditto if you find yourself out in the sun at the park or the beach all day, or doing an intense workout, and nothing else is available. But if you're grocery shopping (and if your water is safe, as we discussed in Part 1), don't make a routine of all the members of the family relying on bottled beverages for daily hydration. This includes not just water but sport drinks, juices, and the like, which aren't good for health anyway.

4 CUT DOWN ON FOODS IN CANS LINED WITH BPA. This means that, when possible, opt for fresh or frozen, or items that come in glass containers (such as tomato sauce in jars instead of cans); for canned products, find brands that are BPA-free (though you'll want to check what material the brand uses to replace that plastic lining).

5 DO A TRIAL RUN. As a starting point, try going plastic-free for just a week or a month; think of giving up single-use plastics for Lent or the month of January, much like people do with red meat or alcohol or added sugar. If nothing else, it will make you aware of all the places in your life where you're relying on single-use plastics.

6 BUY IN BULK. Most health food stores and some larger chain supermarkets like Sprouts and Whole Foods Market have sizable bulk aisles. Buying in bulk can not only save you money but also cut down on your consumption of single-use plastics. Some retailers are even rebranding these as plastic-free aisles. To minimize the use of the bags they have on hand (which, at least, are increasingly compostable), bring your own small reusable bags (cloth, for instance).

7 PICK PLASTIC-FREE POTS. Many home coffee machines have BPA in their tubing or plastic components. Consider using a French press instead.

8 #STOPSUCKING. Think twice before using a straw. If you or someone in your care is disabled and can drink only through a straw, or if you just really prefer to drink beverages through straws, opt for a less harmful material like the many compostable options made of bamboo or hay, or the reusable stainless steel ones. (Paper ones look cute but don't hold up well.)

9 CHOOSE BY NUMBERS. If you look closely at the bottom of a plastic container or plastic bag, you'll typically see a little number inside a triangle. It refers to the type of plastic used and whether it can be recycled in your area. Download the recycling guidelines for plastic in your municipality so you can increase the proportion of your household plastic

RECYCLABLE PLASTIC CHEAT SHEET

SAFEST | LESS SAFE (& HARDER TO RECYCLE)

PETE 1 HDPE 2 PVC 3 PS 6

LDPE 4 PP 5 OTHER 7

diverted from the landfill. Checking that little number on containers can also help you reduce contact with phthalates and BPA. Generally speaking, numbers 1, 2, 4, and 5 are the safest; numbers 3, 6, and 7 are more likely to contain yucky chemicals, and they can also be more difficult to recycle.

10 **IF ALL THIS IS REALLY STRIKING A CHORD, TRY FOR A ZERO-WASTE HOUSEHOLD.** We've been speaking primarily of your use of plastics to transport, store, and serve foods or beverages to you and your family, but of course once you're in the practice of policing your plastic use, you may as well continue reducing it across the board, from cotton swabs with paper stems versus plastic stems to rethinking the disposability of razors, toothbrushes, tampons, and beyond. Zero-waste lifestyle bloggers have books and apps and all kinds of tips and tricks for you to take plastic avoidance as far as you can. And coming to a neighborhood near you . . . no-waste grocery stores. There, you bring your own containers for everything. Toothpaste on tap, chocolate sold packaging-free, even crackers and berries you buy by the scoop.

BULK AISLE BEST PRACTICES

1 **BYOC.** Bring your own container. Cotton drawstring bags work great for dry goods (nuts, legumes, whole grains), and glass jars are perfect for liquids or spreads like olive oil or freshly ground peanut butter. The zero-waste blog *Litterless.com* has a state-by-state database of stores that let you bring containers from home. To avoid paying for the weight of your container, place it on the scale empty before filling it up so you can subtract that amount at the register.

2 **READ THE LABEL.** While you're busy demonstrating eco-citizenship, don't lose sight of the health part of the equation: Just because an item is found in the bulk aisle doesn't mean it's healthy. Cross-reference the Nutrition Facts panel and ingredients list on the bin just as you would for a packaged food.

3 **DO THE MATH.** There are loads of deals to be had in this part of the store, but you'll want to do some quick calculations to avoid sticker shock at checkout—rosemary sea salt cashews, for instance, can cost a pretty penny, whereas plain cashews might be a steal. Maybe it's worth seasoning them yourself at home instead? Or take a simple trail mix of chocolate chips, almonds, and dried cranberries—you're paying a premium for someone to mix those items together, whereas buying the three ingredients from their separate bulk bins will likely be where the savings are.

42

HOW THE HECK DO I READ A FOOD LABEL?

L et's say you've got a food product in your hand, and you're determined to evaluate its merit. Here's how.

STEP I: START WITH THE NUTRITION FACTS PANEL.

WHAT'S LISTED ON THE PANEL

Serving size: The amount of the product typically consumed at once

Calories: The number of calories, or energy, provided by a single serving. A total of 2,000 calories is the daily amount recommended for the average American. To check the number recommended for you personally, use an online calorie calculator. I like the one provided by the Mayo Clinic.

Percent Daily Value: The Daily Value is how much of a given nutrient you should either aim to reach (for example, dietary fiber) or keep below (like sodium). Knowing how much of that amount is in a given food can help you keep track.

Nutrients: Carbohydrates and cholesterol, fats and protein, plus certain vitamins and minerals

INFORMATION TO PAY THE MOST ATTENTION TO
(numbers listed are the daily amounts for an average American adult)

Calories: Most people should shoot for approximately 2,000 a day.

Saturated fat: 20 grams at the most. It's natural to focus on keeping your total intake as low as possible, but give equal concern

UNDERSTANDING THE NUTRITION PANEL

This granola bar gets a pretty good grade—for a processed food.

Nutrition Facts

Serving size	1 bar (35g)

Amount per serving

Calories 150

% Daily Value*

	%
Total Fat 5g	6%
Saturated Fat 1.5g	8%
Trans Fat 0g	
Cholesterol 0mg	0%
Sodium 95mg	4%
Total Carbohydrate 23g	8%
Dietary Fiber 2g	7%
Total Sugars 6g	
Includes 6g Added Sugars	12%
Protein 3g	
Vitamin D	0%
Calcium	2%
Iron	6%
Potassium	2%

INGREDIENTS: Oats, cane sugar, tapioca syrup, canola oil, brown rice, millet, honey, coconut, buckwheat, brown rice flour, amaranth, oat flour, gum acacia, sea salt, quinoa, brown rice syrup, Vitamin E (tocopherols to maintain freshness).
Allergen Information: Contains coconut. Made in a facility that processes peanuts, tree nuts, soy and sesame seeds.

REASONABLE NUMBER GIVEN THE SERVING SIZE IS A FULL GRANOLA BAR.

AIM LOW. THIS IS FINE.

AVOID ALTOGETHER.

SINCE YOU'RE AIMING FOR 25-36 GRAMS TOTAL IN A DAY, 6 ISN'T BAD.

GREAT TO SEE A WHOLE FOOD—AND A WHOLE GRAIN—AS THE FIRST INGREDIENT.

SECOND AND THIRD INGREDIENTS ARE ADDED SWEETENERS, THOUGH. WHILE THE NUTRITION PROFILE OF THIS PRODUCT IS NOT BAD OVERALL, THIS IS CLEARLY A HIGHLY PROCESSED FOOD.

to what you're offsetting the saturated fat with in your diet: Aim for healthy, aka unsaturated, fats (which don't appear on the panel), whole grains, fruits, and vegetables.

Trans fat: 0 grams. Though this type of fat can be found in meat and milk, the majority in the US food supply is the artificial kind, usually in the form of partially hydrogenated oils. Mostly solid at room temperature, trans fat is found in relatively high quantities in margarine, shortening, and processed foods with "partially hydrogenated oils" as an ingredient. Trans fat is no longer "Generally Recognized as Safe" by the FDA. As a result of a call to eradicate artificial sources of trans fat from the US food supply (and a similar mandate worldwide by the World Health Organization), many manufacturers have already removed it from their products, though it looks like it will be mid-2021 before all trans fat is truly eliminated from packaged food. So keep checking those labels.

Sodium: The Daily Value is 2,300 mg. But the American Heart Association, Center for Science in the Public Interest, and Harvard T. H. Chan School of Public Health urge the government to lower its recommendation to 1,500 mg (less than a teaspoon of salt). Our current average sodium intake is roughly 3,400 mg. Yikes! Over 70 percent of that comes from food eaten away from home (processed or prepared foods from the grocery store, or food from restaurants). So, along with added sugar, this is one of the most important things to check on the Nutrition Facts panel.

Added sugar: The Daily Value is 50 grams, but the American Heart Association suggests going much lower, to no more than 25-36 grams:

* **MEN**: 9 teaspoons = 36 grams = 150 calories
* **WOMEN**: 6 teaspoons = 25 grams = 100 calories

I've got quite the sweet tooth myself, so trust me, I know this isn't always easy. A raspberry-flavored salad dressing or simple afternoon cookie can break the bank. So maybe it's no surprise that the average American is actually downing more than 70 grams of added sugar a day.

Dietary fiber: 28 grams. This has been deemed a "nutrient of public health concern." Why the alarm? Fiber is important for maintaining healthy digestion, yet most Americans don't consume nearly enough. Lack of fiber in your diet can lead to constipation and other undesirable bowel problems; not having enough may also keep you from feeling full, which can lead to eating too many calories and possibly gaining weight over time. Fiber is your friend! It's also your gut microbiome's friend. If you're not sold on upping your fiber intake for the sake of living a long and healthy life, do it for the microbes. It's the least any gracious host would do to make them comfortable during their stay. #feedyourgut

OTHER INFORMATION

Total fat: For several years now, after realizing the negative health effects of countless consumers replacing fat in their diets with refined carbs and sugars, nutrition experts have communicated their agreement that the upper limit for total fat should no longer be listed on the panel. It's the type of fat that matters more than the amount. Don't worry about total fat on the label; look to avoid trans fat completely and keep saturated fat as low as possible.

Protein: Other than select groups like teenage girls and the elderly, most people in the United States are getting more than enough protein in their diets just from eating a mix of different foods.

Cholesterol: Although it's still listed on the panel, the consensus among nutrition scientists is that dietary cholesterol (the kind you get from food) is not as much of a concern as it once was. It only minimally affects blood cholesterol levels (which are still quite important to pay attention to), whereas the types of fat you eat affect your blood levels far more.

Carbohydrates: Looking at the Nutrition Facts panel, you won't be able to tell whether the carbs are refined carbs, which you want to keep to a minimum because they jolt your blood sugar much like eating actual sugar does (think white flour), or higher-quality, slower-metabolizing carbs (think fruits, vegetables, whole grains). For that type of information, it's best to check the ingredients list. The other carb-related intel you might gather from the panel would be essentially grams of added sugar (aim low) and dietary fiber (aim high).

STEP 2: READ THE INGREDIENTS LIST.

* Ingredients are listed in descending order by weight.

* You won't see percentages or proportions. This makes it tough to contextualize the amount of each ingredient relative to the others.

* The list must be complete.

* As a general rule, the first ingredient is the most important in the list. Still, it's worth scanning at least the first three ingredients. Look for healthy whole foods (fruits, vegetables, whole grains, nuts, legumes, and the like).

STEP 3: CROSS-REFERENCE THE TWO. PROCEED ACCORDINGLY.

The International Food Information Council Foundation has found that more than half of consumers consult the ingredients list or Nutrition Facts panel often or always before making a food purchasing decision. Cross-referencing them gives you a good overall picture of a product's nutritional value. For example, you might check the amount of added sugar in the Nutrition Facts panel but then consult the ingredients list to see what other company the sugar has—if it's nuts, seeds, whole grains, and so on, as opposed to enriched flour, partially hydrogenated oil, artificial colors, etc., then that sugar might be worth it.

43

HOW TO READ THE FRONT
OF A FOOD PACKAGE

E very item you pick up in the grocery store faces a critical juncture, at which you decide its fate: to remain on the shelf or go home with you. When I enter a grocery store, I often think of movies like *Toy Story*, where the toys are frozen, inanimate objects until the humans leave the room. In the produce section, each item is alive, slowly decaying from the moment it's picked. Its color, texture, size, maybe its smell, speak to us, but ever so quietly. Each one eagerly pines to be selected, to resist the fate of being wasted at store closing. The same goes for fresh baked goods in the bakery, and fish and meat behind the deli counters. Well, minus the part about being alive.

But pretty much all the other products in the supermarket don't merely beckon coyly—they shout at the top of their lungs.

Between the rainbow fonts and the perky cartoon characters, most food packages present a hypnotizing lack of white space only an ink-happy tattoo artist could appreciate. It's no easy task, but by the end of this section, you should know what to make of the puzzle of words and numbers that stands between you and sturdy, self-assured decisions about what to eat.

WHAT'S ON THE FRONT

Labels on the front of a product have one job: persuading you to buy it.

IF YOU LOOK AT THE FACE OF A FOOD PACKAGE, YOU'LL MOST LIKELY FIND THE FOLLOWING:

* The product's brand.

* The product's name—e.g., juice, jam, or jelly; chips, crisps, or crackers. Or maybe that new catchall, "clusters."

* Descriptions of ingredients, flavors, or other attributes the manufacturer has chosen to emphasize.

* Images that help reinforce the description. You might see a glam shot of plump red strawberries for strawberry-flavored yogurt, or a vibrant fresh onion beside a heaping bowl of white fluff for sour-cream-and-onion-flavored chips.

* How much food the product contains, in weight—ounces and grams, typically.

* Occasionally this is also where you'll find food date labels— "sell by," "use by," "best if used by"—though they can be tricky to spot, because the location varies. By and large, these labels indicate quality—optimal freshness and taste, according to the manufacturer—as opposed to food safety. (See "Sell By: The Truth Behind the Date," on page 206.)

YOU MIGHT ALSO SEE

* health claims of various stripes;

* third-party certification labels; and

* some nutrition information that's similar, though not identical, to what's on the Nutrition Facts panel. That is by design.

DISTRACTION TACTICS

Food labeling is an art of sleight of hand and misdirection. Don't get taken by misleading claims. The following are the most common tactics.

Health halos: A "health halo" is a psychological phenomenon in which we perceive a product overall as being healthier and lower in calories when it has one or more labels indicating that something we perceive as bad has been removed—classic examples are "low-fat" and "gluten-free." In reality, those products are typically about the same calorically and the same or worse nutritionally (depending on the replacement ingredients, which are often higher amounts of salt and sugar). As a result, most of us will unwittingly eat more of products like these than we would have of the original product.

Product imagery can have a similar health halo effect. Because most of us are naturally drawn to convenience and novel food products that skew less healthy than their whole-foods ancestors, much effort goes into making foods that aren't too good for us seem good for us. Ever see the product veggie sticks or veggie straws? It's a classic health halo example. On the front you'll see beautiful portraits of spinach and tomatoes, but the first ingredient is actually potato flour. Then farther down the list you'll see some spinach powder or tomato powder. Tricksters! I fell for this myself recently with beet crackers. There was a photo on the front of a racy red beet. Only once I got home did I notice that the first ingredient was actually potato flour. Sure, "beet powder" was second on the list, but it

Garden-to-bag!

VEGETABLE STRAWS*

GLUTEN-FREE AND GUILT-FREE!

Sumptuous straw-based snacking – with produce-inspired shapes and colors!

* JUST, YOU KNOW... MINUS THE ACTUAL... VEGETABLES.

meant the food itself was really a beet-flavored potato chip, not a beet chip.

Despite regulations insisting that imagery not be misleading, the definition of that rule remains rather subjective. Take strawberry-flavored toaster pastries with that strawberry pinup on the box. Then you see that actual strawberries are MIA on the ingredients list. The manufacturer instead essentially made a composite likeness through some pureed apple, Red 40 dye (which contains cancerous compounds, mind you), and artificial strawberry flavor. Nothing against apples, but you probably thought you were diversifying your fruit intake or getting a more premium ingredient in your product.

Emphasizing certain information to make you overlook other information: Sometimes a label on the front will say "0 grams trans fat," but the product actually packs on the saturated fat. Ditto for a product having a product having "No added sugar" while soaring in sodium. This is another reason to routinely flip the product over to check the Nutrition Facts panel.

Another issue may be that the numbers on the front are large, yet it's hard to make out the Percent Daily Value. Like the selectiveness of the facts themselves, this difference from the Nutrition Facts panel also appears to be by design. For instance, 500 mg potassium may sound high, but it's only 14 percent of your Daily Value. Five grams of saturated fat may sound low, but it's 25 percent of your Daily Value, which is actually a lot when tucked into a small amount of food.

USING WORDS THAT ARE TECHNICALLY ALLOWED BUT HAVE LITTLE MEANING
(or a meaning that's not what most of us would expect)

"Reduced": This means the product contains 25 percent less of something—usually sodium or fat—than the original version of that product. It does not mean the amount of that substance is low relative to how much is recommended in a given day. For instance, take a can of soup. The reduced-sodium version could have 870 mg of sodium, whereas the original version had 1,160. That's 25 percent less, so the "low-sodium" option is certainly better, but it's still providing a significant portion of your 2,300 mg daily total.

"Natural": A few years ago, a Consumer Reports survey found that 84 percent of consumers thought the word *natural* on a food label should mean no artificial ingredients or colors or toxic pesticides were used, and 82 percent thought it should mean no genetically modified organisms were used. Surprise! All of these things have been allowed under the term. The problem has been the lack of a formal definition for *natural*. There are innumerable ways to interpret the vague parameters the FDA did have in place, which were that a product wouldn't contain any synthetic or artificial ingredients "that would not normally be expected to be in that food." Thousands of people weighed in through a comment period that ended in 2016, but for the true clarity the public needs, the wait continues. Also problematic is the term *natural flavors*, since a manufacturer doesn't have to specify what those flavors are exactly. If you're trying to avoid certain ingredients—like flavoring agents derived from animals if you're on a vegan diet, or if you have a food allergy—this ambiguity can be quite serious.

Structure/function claims: Ever notice a callout on the package such as "calcium builds strong bones"? That's an example of a structure/function claim. It says that a component in the product has been linked to a certain function in the body. Often these claims distract from unhealthy qualities in the product or are a stretch, to say the least. Since they aren't regulated by the FDA, it's best not to put too much stock in them.

44

UP YOUR SUPERMARKET SAVVY

As you navigate food labels, keep in mind the following over-arching tips:

1 WHENEVER SOMETHING GETS REMOVED FROM A PROCESSED FOOD PRODUCT, IT MUST BE REPLACED WITH SOMETHING ELSE. The replacement item will need to serve a similar function (desired texture, shelf life, flavor, color, and so on). Take gluten-free products, for instance. Gluten provides elasticity and strength to dough, serving as a binder. Commonly, gluten-free products rely on flour substitutes like tapioca starch and rice starch, which are blood-sugar-spiking refined carbs. And sometimes the thing being subbed in may actually be worse for you nutritionally than the thing originally deemed to be bad.

2 KEEP YOUR EYES ON THE PRIZE: YOUR GENERAL HEALTH. Rather than fixating on specific nutrients or trying out strict diets over the short term, the best bet for a lifetime of healthy eating is to enjoy the flavorful and diverse options included in a dietary pattern with lots of evidence behind its long-term health benefits, such as flexitarian eating. In the context of navigating food labels, sometimes you need to pull your head up, take a step back, and keep the bigger picture in mind. Which means remembering that as a rule of thumb, most of the healthiest foods don't even have labels for you to read in the first place.

3 FORTIFYING PROCESSED FOODS DOES NOT MAKE THEM HEALTHY. A common example is enriched grains. Author Warren Belasco has a great term, *nutrification*, that he gives to this surprisingly common practice of a manufacturer taking an ingredient—such as wheat kernels—and removing the most healthy components—the germ and the bran, in this case—to make it easier to turn that ingredient into a highly processed food. The manufacturer will then add back in approximations of the nutritional attributes that would have inherently been in the food—such as iron—so they can tout that supposed value-add on the label, and perhaps even sell the product at a higher price point. Instead, buy foods closer to their original form, like whole-wheat bread or wheat berries, before their most valuable nutritional assets have been removed.

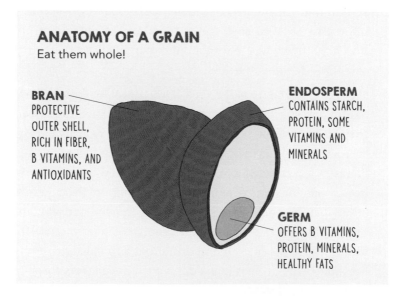

ANATOMY OF A GRAIN
Eat them whole!

BRAN
PROTECTIVE OUTER SHELL, RICH IN FIBER, B VITAMINS, AND ANTIOXIDANTS

ENDOSPERM
CONTAINS STARCH, PROTEIN, SOME VITAMINS AND MINERALS

GERM
OFFERS B VITAMINS, PROTEIN, MINERALS, HEALTHY FATS

45

WHAT TO MAKE OF CALORIES: FOR HEALTH

Much ink has been spilled on whether "a calorie is a calorie," meaning whether your body treats one calorie differently over another depending on its source, i.e., what food it comes from. The short answer is that the distinction does not matter on a cellular level, but it matters very much on many other levels.

To understand what calories are, exactly, I like the explanation given by Dr. Walter Willett in his book *Eat, Drink, and Be Healthy*: "The amount of energy a particular food can deliver to mitochondria—the tiny engines that power your cells—is measured in calories." So, basically, they're like gas in the tank. The bodies of most people eating a mix of foods convert carbohydrates, fats, and protein to energy at the same rate. Calories keep us in forward motion. Or as my summer camp counselors trained us to sing cheerfully at dawn, they keep us *alive, awake, alert, enthusiastic!*

But aside from the essential task of providing energy, food is, of course, far more than fuel. And there are important ways in which calories are different from each other, meaning the equation for nutrition and health goes well beyond the simple math of energy in, energy out. As with most things in life, calories are about both quality and quantity.

In general, calorie quality is more important than just the number in isolation. Where the calories come from translates into more or less nutritional bang for your buck. You might get only 100 calories from a serving of cold cuts on a sandwich, but it would also likely bring along saturated fat, sodium, and colorectal cancer risk. You'd be better off getting 200 calories from an avocado, which would give you beneficial nutrients and fats. Or say you want to spend 100 calories on something to satisfy an afternoon sweet tooth with a snack. Put them toward a soda and you'll experience a blood sugar spike and still be hungry, whereas allocating them to an apple instead will mean a slower absorption of the sugar and feeling full for a while.

And no free passes just because a product is zero-calorie. Take a zero-calorie soda. It's also zero-nutrient. And yet it comes packed with artificial sweeteners, which renders it either negative health-wise or, at best, nutritionally empty.

There's a critical link between how many calories you eat and the quality they contribute to your overall long-term health. When evaluating calories, try to think holistically about the total value of the given food or product: *Will it do me harm? Will it do me good?*

46

WHAT TO MAKE OF CALORIES: FOR THE PLANET

When we talk about calories, it might seem like one of the few times when it's OK to be focused only on our own well-being, with not much to consider in the realm of how it might affect others and the planet. Except: *Producing foods that don't offer much nutritionally is not a very responsible use of natural resources.*

Around the world, we've got a billion hungry people at the same time that we have a billion overweight and obese people. The triple whammy is that one-third of all food produced is lost or wasted. If we recovered just one-fourth of the food currently lost or wasted around the globe, we'd be able to feed all those hungry people—and then some.

Whenever I hear the hyperbole about how on earth we're going to feed 10 billion people by 2050, I think about how much food is also effectively wasted every time it's put into highly processed products that are objectively junk—empty calories, as they're also called. Corn isn't inherently unhealthy; we make it so by turning it into high-fructose corn syrup. Potatoes aren't inherently unhealthy; we make them so by frying them in unhealthy fats and adding heaps of salt and other toppings. And what happens to all the nutrient-filled skins? In other words, the feeding-the-world issue is about how we use the land we have to produce food, and how we use the food we already produce. Consider, for example, that the same acre of land can give us 250 pounds of beef *or* 30,000 pounds of carrots *or* 50,000 pounds of tomatoes. That's based on a still widely referenced study conducted by researchers at the University of California Cooperative Extension in 1978. The issue is also about improving distribution systems to reach those who currently don't have access to nourishing food. Those sticky situations aren't on you to solve personally, but you and your family do have a role to play.

Beyond not wasting the calories and nutrients and deliciousness that come into your possession, here are three problems and solutions for how to make your calorie-related food choices more environmentally responsible.

1   PROBLEM: Foods with high conversion ratios hurt the planet. This is where things get really juicy at the intersection of health and sustainability. It takes approximately 2 calories of feed to produce 1 calorie of fish. By contrast, it requires about 36 calories of feed to produce 1 calorie of beef. This is the concept of "feed conversion efficiency." How efficient is that food at becoming food? The ratio for pork is about 11:1, with poultry not far behind at 9:1. Altogether, according to the book *Eat for the Planet*, it takes 160 times as many land resources to produce beef as it does to grow fruits, vegetables, and legumes. Don't get me started on the high water footprints. Generally speaking, animal-based foods are less efficient uses of natural resources because you're growing animal feed and relying on these creatures to "convert" that feed into food that humans eat, rather than just growing food for humans to eat directly. So, even though a food might be high in nutrients for the high calories it "costs" you, so to speak, its high conversion ratio should give you pause. SOLUTION: Replacing some of the animal-based foods in your diet with plant-based foods is not only good for your body but more environmentally efficient.

FEED CONVERSION EFFICIENCY

This wonky term basically means how many calories of animal feed are required to produce 1 calorie of human food.

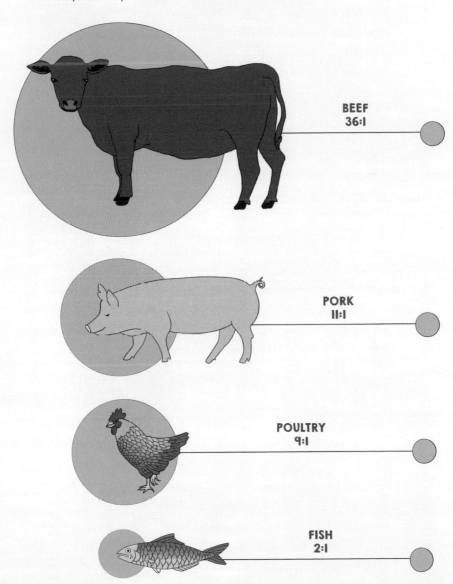

BEEF
36:1

PORK
11:1

POULTRY
9:1

FISH
2:1

2 **PROBLEM:** Foods that are low-calorie can be low- or no-nutrient and high-resource. Approximately one-third of Americans' calories come from "nutrient-poor" foods. When we choose nutrient-poor foods that are also calorie-free or low-calorie, it might seem like a wash. What's the harm? Well, we're still pouring heaps of natural resources into producing essentially useless products. Air-popped chips come to mind, for example. Or take diet soda. A 16.9-ounce bottle might contain zero calories. Bravo. Except it actually involves between 170 and 310 liters of water to make that much soda and deliver it to you in that plastic bottle, according to a figure the Water Footprint Network provided to the *New York Times*. As we know, single-use containers are buggers. For empty calories, think also of all the energy required to produce those foods—the lights to power the factories, the electricity to power the machines, the fuel to drive the trucks or ships to move the large volumes of nutritionally pointless products all around the world. Not to mention the resources required to make the plastic or the cardboard or that silvery lining material of chip bags. All that energy (and land) could have gone into making a nutrient-rich food, maybe even a high-calorie but higher-*quality* food, for someone who needs it. It's situations like these that contribute to the obesity-hunger paradox, which you can think of as two sides of the same coin. **SOLUTION:** Replace nutrient-poor foods (whether packed with calories or not) with nutrient-rich foods—especially those that don't involve a lot of processing and packaging. Both your body and this little planet of ours will thank you.

3 **PROBLEM:** Foods that are high-nutrient, low-calorie, and low-resource are often low-profit, making them a tough economic sell. I'm talking fruits and veggies, unfortunately. Cancer researchers have found a gaping hole between what the US government recommends Americans eat and what US farmers grow. If everyone actually started eating the way experts suggest—reaching the recommended servings of vegetables, legumes, and whole grains—we wouldn't currently have enough supply. To reach our optimal diet quality, we would need to increase the supply of vegetables by 70 percent, double the supply of fruit (mostly whole fruit, since we've got plenty of juice), and quadruple the fraction of the grains that remain whole-grain, rather than get refined. As researchers note, to tip the economic balance we need a big "push" from government, agriculture, marketing, and economic policies. Together, corn and soy make up half the entire US harvest. Most of the varieties grown aren't even edible, because they're used for animal feed, sugar, or oil. Put another way: We don't need farmers to produce more calories, we need them to produce *better* calories.

Consumer demand can provide the "pull" that's needed in parallel. As a consumer, what does that mean to you personally? Vote with your grocery basket. If the rolled oats start flying off shelves, for example, more farmers could become incentivized to plant oats as part of their crop mix. The same goes for manufacturers being compelled to emphasize the more minimally processed options among their product portfolios. For example, as we've already seen, consumers have been buying less and less soda. In response, Pepsi and Coke have shifted more of their focus to water. (We've still got the issue of all the single-use bottles and cans to contend with, but it's a step in the right direction.) SOLUTION: Eating fruits and vegetables and legumes and whole grains is good for your health and requires minimal natural resources to produce; to free up more land to grow calories from those types of foods, contribute to the economic pull by buying ever more of them.

ADDED SUGARS AND ARTIFICIAL SWEETENERS

I f you remember nothing else about sugar and sweetness from this book, remember that the simplest, most healthful goal you can set in this arena is to *keep the amount of added sugar as low as possible.* Although the Daily Value is 50 grams, the American Heart Association recommends keeping it to 25–36 grams per day.

AHA-RECOMMENDED DAILY SUGAR VALUES

Men	9 teaspoons	36 grams	150 calories
Women	6 teaspoons	25 grams	100 calories
Children	3–6 teaspoons (depends on age and caloric needs)	12–25 grams	50–100 calories

Also under the heading of sugar-related "good intention, wrong abstention" is the tendency among many consumers to believe that added sugars that are either naturally derived or zero-calorie are more healthy.

Much marketing has gone into convincing us that anything "natural" must be healthier than something artificial. Some of the naturally derived sugar sources like agave nectar and maple syrup do have nutrients, whereas all the nutrients have been stripped out of table sugar. But you'd have to consume unhealthy quantities of those natural sweeteners to reap any health benefits, so it's a moot point. *Added sugars behave basically the same way in the body, whether we're talking about white sugar,*

SUGAR'S 61 PSEUDONYMS

In the cast of food ingredients that make up processed foods, sugar is a character by many names: sixty-one in total, according to the University of California, San Francisco's estimate. Often small amounts of several different types of sugar—from maltose to molasses and agave nectar to corn syrup—are listed separately in an ingredients list on a food package to avoid one large total amount landing at the beginning of the list.

MUSCOVADO CORN SYRUP MOLASSES CANE SUGAR BARLEY MALT
MALTOSE BEET SUGAR DATE SUGAR
FRUIT JUICE CONCENTRATE
CANE JUICE CRYSTALS PALM SUGAR BUTTERED SYRUP
SORGHUM SYRUP DEXTRIN
EVAPORATED CANE JUICE CORN SYRUP SOLIDS
COCONUT PALM SUGAR FRUIT JUICE BROWN SUGAR
GLUCOSE SOLIDS
CAROB SYRUP AGAVE NECTAR GLUCOSE
CARAMEL MALTOL FREE-FLOWING BROWN SUGARS
COCONUT SUGAR DEHYDRATED CANE JUICE
SYRUP HONEY SWEET SORGHUM ICING SUGAR
BARLEY MALT SYRUP GRAPE SUGAR INVERT SUGAR
CORN SWEETENER MAPLE SYRUP TREACLE
CANE JUICE RAW SUGAR DEXTROSE MANNOSE
REFINER'S SYRUP BARBADOS SUGAR CASTOR SUGAR
GOLDEN SYRUP CONFECTIONERS' SUGAR MALT SYRUP
TURBINADO SUGAR FRUCTOSE GOLDEN SUGAR
YELLOW SUGAR SUCROSE POWDERED SUGAR
SUGAR (GRANULATED) DEMERARA SUGAR
HFCS (HIGH-FRUCTOSE CORN SYRUP)
RICE SYRUP
SACCHAROSE MALTODEXTRIN PANOCHA

brown sugar, corn syrup, evaporated cane juice, agave nectar, and so on. One exception—what you might call a slightly less bad option, which is relevant only if you're replacing table sugar as opposed to consuming it in addition—is honey. The main reason is its antioxidant content. Though higher in calories by tablespoon than table sugar, honey's goopy consistency and higher concentration of sweetness means you may be inclined to use less of it.

What we know about added sugar: Consuming too much over the long run can lead to weight gain. Eating sugar raises blood sugar levels, which prompts the pancreas to release insulin; raised insulin levels prompt the body to store more of our calories from food as fat. There are also hormonal changes. Leptin, our "I'm-full" hormone, gets essentially drowned out by insulin levels that are out of whack, so we eat more and potentially gain weight. Some studies suggest that sugar has an addictive effect on us, much like a drug, in which our brain chemistry changes; we crave sugar, need it in our minds as a reward, and experience withdrawal-type symptoms without it. Finally, it's more than just weight gain and hormone changes at stake: Over time, overconsuming added sugar has been linked to numerous metabolic problems, which together have been dubbed "metabolic syndrome." These chronic conditions can greatly increase the likelihood of heart disease and diabetes, and they top the list of common causes of death. Oh, and cavities. Remember those?

What we don't know about added sugar: We don't know whether consuming too much over the long run is *also* tied to accelerated aging of our cells (which appears most visibly as wrinkles), memory loss and Alzheimer's disease, and the increased incidence of some cancers, including rates of survival and recurrence among patients who have already endured cancer treatment. The science is too young in these areas to say conclusively, but for now, early studies suggest ties.

What we know about artificial sweeteners: They may lead us to consume more food in total because they appear to interfere with our internal calorie detectors. This happens because sweetness triggers our brains to say, "Eat more!" And artificial sweeteners are often hundreds of times sweeter than sugar. Artificial sweeteners may also lead us to seek more sweet foods and drinks overall because they train our palates to prefer sweetness—to be sugar dependent, even—and because they provide sweetness without calories. (Artificial sweeteners don't appear to trigger the same reward response we get from added sugars.) Lastly, because they're *so* sweet, they may also cause naturally sweet foods like fruit to be less satisfying when we crave sweetness.

What we don't know about artificial sweeteners: A lot. It's basically a battle between the FDA and the Center for Science in the Public Interest.

"GENERALLY RECOGNIZED AS SAFE" BY THE FDA:
* advantame
* aspartame (Equal/NutraSweet)
* acesulfame potassium (Ace-K)
* luo han guo (also called monk fruit) extracts
* neotame
* saccharin (Sweet'N Low)
* steviol glycosides
* sucralose (Splenda)

INGREDIENTS TO AVOID FROM THE CENTER FOR SCIENCE IN THE PUBLIC INTEREST:

* aspartame (Equal/NutraSweet)
* acesulfame potassium (Ace-K)
* luo han guo (also called monk fruit) extracts
* saccharin (Sweet'N Low)
* steviol glycosides
* sucralose (Splenda)

As you can see, the only ingredients the CSPI allows are advantame and neotame. On its website, the National Cancer Institute concludes that the studies for aspartame, saccharin, and sucralose do not present enough evidence to associate them with cancer risk. (Separately, there are also some questions about the safety of artificial sweeteners for pregnant women, and sucralose has been suspected as potentially degrading the health of the gut microbiome.)

What to make of it all? With so much up in the air about artificial sweeteners, I say better the devil you know. Keep added sugar to a minimum and check the ingredients list to be sure you spot all the sources. Many products labeled as having no sugar added may instead have sugar alcohols or artificial sweeteners.

48

LIMITING ADDED SUGAR

The final entry in our log of sugar-related "good intention, wrong abstention" is taking sugar avoidance to such extremes that you miss out on some of life's greatest pleasures.

The biggest problem with added sugars in the American diet is the ubiquity in the food supply. An estimated three-fourths of all packaged foods have had sugar added by manufacturers. In turn, our palates have grown so primed for sweetness that we require greater and greater amounts of sweet to truly taste it. If you've ever experimented with a no-added-sugar rule for yourself, you'll notice after just a week how incredible a ripe, fresh tomato tastes, or that biting into a grape provides an explosion of satisfying sweetness. Eating a peach can be pure bliss, and never before had you thought of carrots as candy. Reacquainting your taste buds with the natural sweetness from whole foods, especially fruits and vegetables, is one of many great reasons to seriously drop your added-sugar intake.

But in doing so, I urge you to not go off the deep end. It doesn't have to be all or nothing to reap the majority of the benefits. For a more sustainable approach, channel your energy toward catching the irksome ways added sugar has crept into foods we wouldn't expect—from

yogurt and juice to soups and sauces, from condiments and cereal to sandwich bread and protein bars. Who wants to blow their sugar budget on soup?

So, look to those processed foods and the not-even-sweet-tasting high-sugar foods as the first places to start slashing your sugar. Cut back on added sugar without being maniacal about it; there's a lot of deliciousness and joy to be experienced in your lifetime, much of which can involve sweets. A fresh-baked summer cobbler. Made-with-love Sunday morning pancakes. Homemade holiday cookies. The adrenaline rush of discovery as you soak up the myriad concoctions of cultures other than your own, whether in your own neighborhood, road-tripping around the United States, or traveling abroad.

If you're cutting down on added sugars in other places in your diet, and treating dessert as the treat it's meant to be—a few times a week at most—then you'll probably have the added-sugar budget left over to enjoy some of the simple pleasures in life.

49

SAFE VS. SCARY INGREDIENTS

The swell of interest in clean labels stems from good intentions—the pursuit of real food. Guidance to seek out foods whose back panels don't read like chemistry textbooks has been about urging Americans to eat more wholesome whole foods. Amen to that! But as convenience wins time and again in our food culture, what has actually come about is a reciprocal tidal wave of "clean-label" packaged foods. They tout their short lists of short-lettered ingredients. It's great that so many of us are giving a closer eye to labels and questioning whether we really want to be putting Red 40 or sucralose in our bodies. But there's a risk in letting that skepticism spill into blanket avoidance of ingredients that are unfamiliar sounding. Ditto for blanket acceptance of ingredients that are nice sounding.

Here are five examples of ingredients that sound scary but are actually safe, and five that sound safe but are actually scary.

SOUND SCARY, ACTUALLY SAFE

1 ASCORBIC ACID. Also known as vitamin C, it helps preserve food's color and flavor.

2 CITRIC ACID. Found in citrus fruits and berries, it's used to add tart flavor.

3 MODIFIED FOOD STARCH. Most commonly made from corn, wheat, potato, or tapioca, these starches have been altered to attain properties desirable in processed foods, such as longer shelf life and stabilization. Usually used as a

thickening agent, like in soups and frozen foods. Remember that safe does not equal healthy.

4 CELLULOSE. A plant fiber found in abundance in nature and used to prevent caking (though some Parmesan cheese makers used it fraudulently as filler in products that were supposedly 100 percent Parmesan). It boosts the fiber content in processed foods but in ways that aren't as beneficial as fiber in whole foods.

5 TOCOPHEROL. Also known as vitamin E, it prevents foods like vegetable oils and breakfast cereals from going rancid.

SOUND SAFE, ACTUALLY SCARY

1 AGAVE NECTAR. Same basic effect on your body as other forms of added sugar. (Meaning, best in moderation.)

2 SEA SALT. Same basic effect on your body as other forms of added salt. (Meaning, best in moderation.)

3 NATURAL FLAVORS. Also known as whatever the manufacturer wants it to mean. A common one that skates by under this more friendly-sounding name is the synthetic emulsifier called "propylene glycol." Not the first thing that comes to mind when you hear "natural." More concerningly, some people are allergic to it and should avoid it.

4 ALOE VERA. Fine for putting on your sunburn, not great to eat. A host of digestive and blood sugar issues have been associated with oral intake.

5 CARAMEL COLORING. If the sugar content weren't enough, the coloring—which is best known in soda but is also used to darken other food products like beer, chocolate-flavored baked goods, and meats—is created by heating with ammonium compounds, the result of which has been deemed a probable carcinogen by the World Health Organization.

These ten ingredients are just a sampling to give you an idea of how nuanced the clean-eating quest can be with respect to packaged foods. That's why true clean eating means reliance on real, whole foods. There's more to learn as you decipher those foods that aren't, so check out a resource called "Chemical Cuisine," published by the Center for Science in the Public Interest. This is a useful list of all the major food additives and their corresponding safety rating, from "safe" and "caution" to "cut back," "certain people should avoid," and "avoid."

6 INGREDIENTS TO WATCH

Aside from Center for Science in the Public Interest's three "terrible" ingredients to avoid—salt, sugar, trans fat—here are six others they'd put under patrol.

FOOD DYES (BLUE 1, BLUE 2, GREEN 3, RED 3, RED 40, YELLOW 5, YELLOW 6)
REASON: SUSPECTED TIES TO CANCER AS WELL AS ADHD

ASPARTAME
REASON: SUSPECTED TIES TO CANCER

ACESULFAME-POTASSIUM
REASON: SUSPECTED TIES TO CANCER, THOUGH DATA IS LIMITED

BHA
REASON: SUSPECTED TIES TO CANCER

SACCHARIN
REASON: SUSPECTED TIES TO CANCER

CAFFEINE
REASON: SUSPECTED TIES TO INSOMNIA, ANXIETY, REDUCED FERTILITY, AND WORSE WHEN CONSUMED IN SUPPLEMENT FORM AND POSSIBLY ENERGY DRINKS. THAT SAID, COFFEE HAS BEEN TIED TO HEALTH BENEFITS, IN FACT, AND FOR MOST PEOPLE, THE AMOUNT OF CAFFEINE IN A REGULAR CUP OR TWO IS TOTALLY HARMLESS.

SELL BY:
THE TRUTH BEHIND THE DATE

I n terms of food safety or health risks, it's generally fine to eat foods past the "sell by," "use by," and "best if used by" dates listed on packages. Almost always, these labels are food manufacturers' suggestions for peak freshness and taste, not expiration dates. In other words, they're about quality, not safety. The labels can be confusing, though, because the definitions of the terms aren't standardized, and labeling practices tend to differ from one product to another and from one manufacturer to another.

There's usually quite a bit more time remaining on the clock than the labels would have you believe. In general, most foods can be eaten days, weeks, or even *months* past those printed dates. Though over generations, many of us have lost the confidence to trust our instincts on whether food is spoiled, we're actually wired with pretty sophisticated detectors. By that I mean our five senses. You take a look at a food and see if it has grown mold or appears slimy, for example, or you take a whiff and notice an off smell. Mold is a serious spoilage issue because it can produce toxins.

Foodborne illness usually happens not because of decay or aging, a natural process, but when there's contamination by a pathogen on a farm or at a processing plant. Pay the most attention to label dates for the same foods that are considered unsafe for pregnant women: deli meats, unpasteurized dairy products, ready-to-eat refrigerated foods, and hot dogs and sausages that aren't fully cooked. The reason these are high-risk is that they may harbor listeria, which unlike most bacteria can grow under refrigeration.

To address consumer confusion and reduce waste, a bill was introduced in Congress in 2016 called the Food Date Labeling Act. It seeks to create a uniform national date labeling system with just two labels: one for quality, i.e., "best if used by," and one for safety, i.e., "expires on." Last I checked, the bill hadn't gained traction, but a two-label system making the important quality-safety distinction would almost certainly cut down on wasted food and wasted money.

Thankfully, most of the big food manufacturers have in the meantime gotten on board with a two-date system of their own, through voluntary guidelines. Put forward by their big lobbying bodies, the Food Marketing Institute and the Grocery Manufacturers Association, the press release reads as follows:

> The new voluntary initiative streamlines the myriad date labels on consumer products packaging down to just two standard phrases. **"BEST If Used By"** describes product quality, indicating that the product may not taste or perform as expected but is safe to use or consume. **"USE By"** applies to the few products that are highly perishable and/or have a food safety concern over time; these products should be consumed by the date listed on the package—and disposed of after that date.

It's still not *quite* as straightforward as we consumers might expect, but it makes a heck of a lot more sense than the ten different dates we've been scratching our heads at all these years.

 LOOK IT UP: For lots of tricks on food storage, check out the directory at *savethefood.com*, a public service campaign sponsored by the Natural Resources Defense Council and the Ad Council.

3 WAYS TO CONSUME WITH CONFIDENCE ANY FOODS IN THE IFFY ZONE:

1 Use the sniff test for milk. If it doesn't smell like it should, don't drink it or mix it in anything.

2 You can tell if eggs are OK to eat by placing one in a bowl of water. If it floats, it's bad; if it sinks, it's good.

3 If you spot browning on foods like avocados and bananas, or if you spot mold on hard cheeses, you can cut those parts off and eat the rest of the product. For cheeses that are soft, shredded, crumbled, or sliced, though, this doesn't work, because the mold can spread throughout the cheese.

BAD   GOOD

51

FOOD LABELS AND ALLERGIES: WHAT TO LOOK FOR

For individuals with food allergies, small amounts of trace ingredients can cause serious symptoms or even be life-threatening.

Know what to look for: Ninety percent of food allergies in the United States are attributed to the top eight most common allergens:

crustacean shellfish // eggs // fish // cow's milk // peanuts // soy // tree nuts // wheat

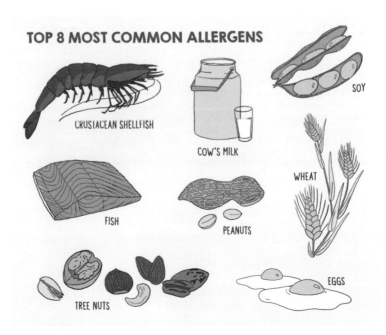

TOP 8 MOST COMMON ALLERGENS

CRUSTACEAN SHELLFISH

COW'S MILK

SOY

FISH

PEANUTS

WHEAT

TREE NUTS

EGGS

Know where to look: As required by the FDA, manufacturers must list any of the top eight allergens their products contain. You'll see this on the ingredients list and/or a note below the list. For example, "whey (milk)" might be noted in the ingredients list, or a note near the list might say "Contains: milk."

Take extra caution with food products outside FDA regulation: For products that are regulated by the USDA instead of the FDA—such as meat and poultry, along with some egg products—allergen labeling is not required. Sure, you might see voluntary advisories on the packaging about a product having been processed in a facility where an allergen was present, but that wouldn't be a guarantee that the product is safe for you or someone in your care with a serious food allergy.

Bottom line: The closer a food or ingredient is to its natural state, the more transparency you generally have about its safety as far as allergens are concerned. Cooking from scratch as much as possible can help. But since few among us have the bandwidth to make every meal with raw ingredients, find your go-to brands and items, and stick with the packaged foods you can trust.

52

IS GLUTEN REALLY THAT BAD?

The cultural explosion of self-diagnosed gluten sensitivity—when it started becoming something your friend would show up at a restaurant telling you about—can be tied to the runaway success of two books. Both deemed gluten a toxin to be eradicated. First, in 2011, Dr. William Davis, with *Wheat Belly*. Then, Dr. David Perlmutter, in 2013, with *Grain Brain*. Who wouldn't shudder in the face of statements like this (from the latter): "Gluten isn't just an issue for those with bona fide celiac disease, an autoimmune disorder that strikes a small minority. As many as 40 percent of us can't properly process gluten, and the remaining 60 percent could be in harm's way. The question we need to be asking ourselves is: *What if we're all sensitive to gluten from the perspective of the brain?*" Davis and Perlmutter were suggesting that going gluten-free had the potential to cure nearly all our woes, from skin discoloration and obesity to depression, schizophrenia, arthritis, and beyond. Hordes of people suddenly went gluten free. No more pastries, cookies, cereal, beer. Maybe the authors were right, but, then again, who wouldn't be feeling like a million bucks after that kind of purge? Word spread like wildfire, likely fueled by that deeply ingrained element of the American food psyche—exceptionalism. The underlying message that rang out was, "Hey, friend/colleague/cousin/

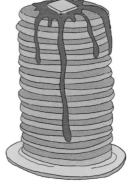

neighbor—you don't even realize how bad you feel. But you deserve to be the best version of you; going gluten-free can help you get there. I tried it myself, and I feel amazing."

In reality, far more of us avoid gluten than need to. About 1 percent of Americans have celiac disease, which is a serious autoimmune disorder. Those people are advised to strictly follow a gluten-free diet. Another 6 percent or so have non-celiac gluten sensitivity, a milder condition tied to digestive problems and other symptoms that does not result in a positive test for celiac disease; observing whether symptoms improve after a trial elimination of gluten is the main method of diagnosis. For *everyone else*, a gluten-free diet is not advised by nutrition experts. Still, a 2013 report by the NPD Group, a market research firm, found that as many as one in three Americans were trying to avoid gluten. That's more Americans than have a gym membership or can name all three branches of government.

SOME UNINTENDED RISKS AND CONSEQUENCES OF GOING GLUTEN-FREE WITHOUT MEDICAL NECESSITY:

Risky replacement ingredients. Once the gluten in a processed food product gets removed, it typically needs to be replaced. And the junk fillers replacing gluten are usually blood-sugar-spiking refined flours such as tapioca starch, potato starch, or rice starch. One large US study found that people on a gluten-free diet had double the arsenic and mercury levels of those who ate gluten. The top suspect? Rice. Now, rice is not inherently bad, but again, the dose makes the poison. As we know, cutting out one thing in the diet almost always means replacing it with something else. Gluten abstainers should consider whether replacement foods are in fact less hazardous.

Salt and sugar overload. Comparisons of gluten-free foods with equivalent products that contain gluten show that the former often have more sugar and salt than the latter. Researchers at the University of Hertfordshire in the United Kingdom evaluated hundreds of products across ten food categories and found that higher salt was consistent among the gluten-free versions; gluten-free breads and flour products were especially likely to have more sugar than the regular versions, whereas differences weren't as noteworthy for gluten-free crackers. Not to mention, gluten-free products in the study tended to have less fiber than the regular versions.

The products cost more. That UK study found that gluten-free products were 159 percent pricier than the regular versions.

Missing out on the health benefits of whole grains. High intake of whole grains—many of which contain gluten—has been associated with reduced risk of heart disease, some cancers, type 2 diabetes, obesity, and death from numerous causes, including infections and respiratory diseases. For many people, going gluten-free means going grain-free, which means going whole-grains-free. Whole grains aren't the only way to get your fiber, but they're a widely available one. As we recall, most of us aren't reaching the daily recommendation of about 28 grams a day on average; it's not that gluten eaters are getting the recommended amount of whole grains and fiber either, but avoiding gluten makes it ever more likely that you'll miss out on those protective benefits.

Bottom line: Talk to your doctor before going gluten-free. Be sure, because the cons may outweigh the pros. Otherwise, free yourself of the supposed woes of enjoying foods with gluten; unless you don't have a choice, skip the headache, health risks, and added cost.

53

MEAL KITS: THINKING INSIDE THE BOX

T he first time I used a meal kit delivery service, I was mortified. Not by how the meal turned out. Not by my ignorance of some of the spices involved. But by the pile of packaging that had been required to get all the ingredients to my house. As a San Francisco Bay Area resident, I waited till dark to take it all out to the garbage bin so my neighbors wouldn't see.

Anyone who has used a meal kit—we're talking Blue Apron, Plated, HelloFresh, Sun Basket, and countless others—has likely faced a similar conundrum: *I feel good about the choice I'm making from a health perspective, but bad about it from an environmental perspective.* Between the pre-portioned baggies of paprika and the plastic-wrapped leaves of basil, along with the heavy-duty cooler packs and insulated bubble liners, the eco-guilt can be crippling. It can feel like you're solving one problem in your life while creating a new one.

To determine what to make of meal kits and whether to incorporate them into your weekly routine, let's compare them to other plausible avenues to dinner and see which road might be the most conscious.

ROUND I: MEAL KIT VS. EATING AT A RESTAURANT

Most often what we order away from home isn't nearly as good for us as what we might eat when preparing a meal ourselves. A meal kit wins for health because it's undoubtedly a more reasonable portion of food, it more likely has a purer set of ingredients—thanks in part to one of the greatest selling points of meal kits, which is the transparency you gain into what you're eating—and it's potentially cooked in a way that's healthier. (Most people don't have deep-fat fryers at home, for instance.)

To truly assess this as a fair fight, we'll assume you're picking both a meal kit company and a restaurant committed to environmental and social responsibility in terms of sourcing and operations. So it comes down to packaging. The degree to which you can recycle all the plastic sub-components of meal kits varies widely, and my experience is that most of it winds up in the trash. The gel packs and insulation usually can't be recycled at all. Then there's all the cardboard, which takes a lot of resources to produce. So, the restaurant wins for sustainability—if you actually eat your leftovers, that is, to avoid food waste.

WINNER: It's a tie

ROUND 2: MEAL KIT VS. TAKEOUT

The breakdown regarding healthy eating for takeout is the same as for restaurant eating—i.e., the meal kit will likely have better portions, better food, and better preparation.

Environmentally, it comes down to comparing packaging and delivery modes. Depending on whether you're driving to pick up your takeout or getting it by some other means, or if you're using a delivery app like GrubHub or Caviar, both takeout and meal kit potentially involve vehicles traveling roughly the same distance, but this wouldn't make much of

a difference in the total equation. At least with takeout you don't need all the infrastructure to keep the ingredients chilled, and some municipalities let you compost take-out containers, but how many people actually know the ins and outs of their waste management company? They're likely getting tossed. Takeout often comes in plastic bags, sometimes with sub-components in similarly wasteful packaging, like individually sized packets of soy sauce that you don't use, or lots of separate containers for separate items. All in all, it seems a wash on sustainability—both are equally wasteful. So the winner is only health, with the meal kit taking this one.

WINNER: Meal kit

ROUND 3: MEAL KIT VS. PLANNING A WEEK OF MEALS AND SHOPPING ONCE

The meals in the meal kit may be healthier and/or more balanced than what you'd pick to make on your own, though it depends on which service and which program you select, and the same goes for the environmental and social responsibility comparison.

But the biggest reason that regular cooking is the better option is the overarching question of being a direct participant in the food system. A critical layer of conscious eating gets lost in the meal kit transition: selecting your ingredients. This book is about practical choices but also about aspirational living, and although not that many people actually plan all their meals and shop once a week anymore, that approach wins: Health and environment are comparable, but planning and shopping keeps you connected to where food comes from and the people behind it—talking to farmers at the farmers' market, say, or doing your homework on which producers to support with your grocery dollars in terms of animal welfare and labor practices. With meal kits, you don't get to make all of those critical choices. Part of the convenience you're paying a premium for is putting the ingredient decision-making in the hands of someone else.

WINNER: Planning and shopping

ROUND 4: MEAL KIT VS. RECIPES WHOSE LEFTOVER INGREDIENTS GET WASTED

We all know the feeling. The moldy tub of sour cream that I used one dollop of for Taco Tuesday, the three-year-old chili powder collecting dust in my spice cabinet. Consider this the environmental dark side of the above scenario. Part of the reason this happens is that grocery items come in packages that are larger than the amount we need. Translation: Not our fault. There are ways around it, like loving the bulk aisle, but most products aren't available that way.

A study by the University of Michigan found that the total carbon footprint of meal kits was way lower compared with the same meal from ingredients purchased at a grocery store. The biggest reason is that, as mentioned, reducing food waste is the third most effective solution for reducing global warming. Packaging matters for environmental impact, to be sure, but food waste matters more. In the study, the greenhouse gas (GHG) emissions for an average meal kit dinner were one-third less than emissions from one made from store-bought ingredients. That's a huge difference, and it especially adds up when we're talking about a habit as frequent as weeknight dinner.

The other part of the problem is that most of us just don't cook that often. On average, Americans spend the least amount of time of any of the major developed countries eating. (We eat a lot of food, but we just eat it really fast.) We also spend the least amount of time cooking. It's one of the great contradictions of the food movement—that for all our apparently heightened interest in food (interest that's a chief content provider to Instagram, the Food Network, Yelp, and the like), we actually haven't matched that enthusiasm by making more of our food at home. Compared with even just a few years ago and certainly with many years ago, we dine out more, order delivery more, and generally outsource more of our meal making to the food and food-service industries. Overwork edges out time that might have been spent on other elements of living, including preparing and enjoying food. The trouble with planning meals for the week is that for many of us, it never pans out. You end up working late, getting hangry, and stopping at Chipotle on your way home before you nose-dive into bed, or any of a dozen scenarios you're probably familiar with. The best intentions give way to food waste when reality meets aspiration in the grind of workweek cooking.

WINNER: Meal kit

ROUND 5: MEAL KIT VS. STOPPING IN THE GROCERY STORE ON THE WAY HOME FROM WORK AND TRYING TO REMEMBER INGREDIENTS FOR A MEAL EVERYONE MIGHT EAT AND ENDING UP WITH PASTA AGAIN

Consider this the nutritional dark side of the above scenario. It's because of how many people lack either command of a kitchen—the confidence to routinely whip up a nutritious, responsible, tasty meal for their family—or the passion for meal planning day after day. In this case, at least you're likely wasting less because you're buying the ingredients the day of. (They're fresher and so probably taste better, too, for what it's worth.) But the quality of the meals becomes questionable when you lack inspiration. Anecdotally, meal kit companies may be nudging people to shift toward healthier, more environmentally friendly eating patterns over the long run. One HelloFresh user told me that seeing the vegetarian-themed option appear in her account interface enabled her and her meat-loving husband to go meatless on the three nights a week they use the service. In other words, meal kits have a way of normalizing certain types of eating, which could go a long way toward shifting our food culture for the better.

WINNER: Meal kit

TALLYING IT ALL TOGETHER: MEAL KITS EDGE OUT OTHER LIKELY DINNER HABITS

If meal kits call to you, and you can afford their high per-person cost—usually still lower than comparable takeout or dining out, but not as cheap as regular cooking—here are some ideas for giving them an even greater upper hand:

* Choose the services that use better packaging. Look for reusability, recyclability, compostability, and less packaging overall. The website *themealkitreview.com* has a nice breakdown of the most "eco-friendly" meal kit companies. Its ranking: Green Chef, HelloFresh, and Sun Basket as the top three.

* Choose services that are transparent about their sourcing. Do they support women-owned businesses? Organic? Fair trade? Local farmers? Meat from animals raised without antibiotics? Sustainable seafood? BPA-free packaging? Decide what values you would most want reflected in the ingredients if you were buying them yourself—these companies are now your grocery shopping proxies, after all.

* Give the vegetarian or vegan plans a whirl. You'll be lowering your environmental footprint while you vary your patterns.

✱ Recognize that meal kits are a trade-off: They save you time, but you are one step removed from the source. When using meal kit services, do what you can to stay connected to the sources of your food. For example, save the recipe cards and remember that you've already successfully cooked that meal, then go buy or order the ingredients yourself. Try alternating weeks: meal kits for those when you have really busy stretches at work versus regular cooking during those that are lighter.

TOP 5 TAKEAWAYS

1 When evaluating packaged foods, do a mental check of three elements:
- the food *in* the package,
- the words *on* the package, and
- the package itself.

2 For sustainable packaging, try for bulk and reusable containers versus single-use ones whenever possible; for you, others, and the planet, glass is the best type of container.

3 To read food labels, focus on two things:
- the ingredients list (first ingredient = most important); and
- the Nutrition Facts panel (keep added sugar, sodium, and unhealthy fats as low as possible).

4 When it comes to calories, both quantity and quality matter—for both human and environmental well-being.

5 Cutting out one thing in the diet almost always means replacing it with something else. The same goes for ingredients in processed foods. Ask yourself whether the replacements are in fact better.

MENU

PART 4

STUFF THAT'S MADE IN RESTAURANT KITCHENS

T ables from reclaimed wood and napkins from unwanted fabric. LED lightbulbs and frying oil turned into biodiesel. Locally sourced everything. To help you look under the hood before you dine somewhere, this section recommends ways to pick the healthiest, most environmentally responsible, most socially conscious restaurants.

Throughout Part 4, keep in mind that by *restaurant*, I mean anywhere you eat away from home, where the food is made by professionals. Restaurants worth investigating are those you patronize most frequently—the twice-a-week sandwich spot on your lunch break, the delivery pizza place for Friday family movie night, the coffee shop where you stop on autopilot each afternoon. Or maybe you work in an academic, health care, or corporate setting where selecting food from a cafeteria is a regular part of your day. Whether it's a slice of pizza at the Costco checkout area, a breakfast sandwich at the Arby's drive-thru, a casual weekend lunch at Panera, or a splurge dinner somewhere special, we now spend more money at bars and restaurants than on foods from the grocery store. In 2015, we hit this milestone for the first time in American history. So, it's not enough to make conscious food decisions about the items in your grocery basket. This final section of the book can help you make conscious choices when dining out: helping you select where to go in the first place to support your own well-being and that of your family, as well as the environment, animals, and restaurant workforce.

In an average day in America, about a third of kids and adults eat at a fast food place. The official term is *limited service* restaurant, meaning you order and pay before you eat, in an environment that may or may not have tables, where you can take it to go or have it delivered. These include both fast food and fast casual restaurants. The latter are characterized by fast service, upscale décor, medium price points, and generally high quality and more transparent sourcing and preparation. *Full-service* restaurants, on the other hand, what you might call "sit-down" restaurants, are those with waiters and a slower pace, a nicer ambience, and higher cost. They're more for special occasions, maybe once a month versus multiple times a week.

In my day job, I work to support the restaurant and food-service industries and help make their menus healthier and better for the environment. I love my work and believe in it. But research consistently shows that meals we make ourselves are most often better for us. They're generally cheaper, too. And they give us greater control and transparency over what we put in our bodies. So, whenever you're choosing a restaurant, keep that broader context in the back of your mind.

54

"HEALTHY" FAST FOOD

To dive into conscious eating away from home, let's start with the sticky business of picking a fast food or fast casual restaurant to optimize the health of you and your family. Here are the main considerations:

Calories and portion size. Excessive portion size is the flip side of the food waste coin. Consider posted calorie counts as one clue for evaluating a given food establishment. Depending on the day, the meal, the snack, or the beverage, and whether you're looking for a little or a lot calorie-wise, having the information can at least ensure you're making the choice intentionally, rather than mindlessly.

Nutritious menu options. There's no definitive "healthiest fast food chains" ranking, but many lifestyle publications provide lists of their own. As a general rule, I'm inclined to trust those backed by registered dietitians, on staff or otherwise. From a culinary standpoint, I tend to agree with the lists of healthiest fast food chains provided by the Food Network and *The Daily Meal*. I also mostly agree with the benchmark for "healthy" used by each one, based purely on the anecdotal experience of having eaten at most of the places on the lists.

The following regional and national chains—which admittedly are all fast casual versus fast food and therefore not as affordable as, say, a drive-thru burger chain—appear on one or both of these lists: Asian Box, Cava Grill, Chopt, Freshii, Modern Market, Noodles & Company, sweetgreen, Tender Greens, Veggie Grill, and Zoë's Kitchen.

Absence of antibiotics in the meat supply. If you're dining at a restaurant or food-service venue that doesn't specify on the menu or in-store marketing materials whether the meat served comes from animals raised without medically important antibiotics, don't be shy about asking your server or at the counter. Think that's too awkward to be realistic? Here's a hypothetical scene: "Excuse me, is the burger/carnitas burrito/kung pao chicken made from animals raised without antibiotics?" "Uh . . . I don't know." "OK—would you mind asking the manager? Thanks!" Even if the manager doesn't have the answer for you on the spot, you can leave feeling good about having done your part to help normalize this kind of transparency. If enough conscious eaters ask, it'll become standard practice to disclose this information in-store or on the company website. And then you won't have to ask anymore; your future self thanks you for enduring a possibly awkward moment.

Each year, in conjunction with other research and advocacy groups, Consumer Reports releases an antibiotic scorecard, "Chain Reaction," evaluating the largest fast food and fast casual brands in America. Beef production takes up 40 percent of the antibiotics important to human medicine that are used by the overall meat industry, whereas chicken takes up just 6 percent. Given beef's large antibiotic footprint, in 2018 Consumer Reports began releasing a separate scorecard just for burger joints. Consult both scorecards before selecting a chain restaurant. (You can find them at *consumerreports.org*.)

On the 2018 burger scorecard, a mere two of the top twenty-five burger chains in America—BurgerFi and Shake Shack—got A grades, meaning 100 percent of the beef they serve is raised without the routine use of antibiotics. More disturbing, twenty-two of the remaining twenty-three got an F grade, meaning they have no substantial antibiotic-reduction policy in place for beef. On the bright side, things can change quickly. The first overall scorecard—which looks at all types of meat that a company serves, namely beef, pork, chicken, and turkey—in 2015 revealed that only five of the top twenty-five chains had policies for reducing antibiotics in any type of meat; by the 2018 overall scorecard, eighteen of twenty-five chains had policies. Consistent star performers since the first report, Panera and Chipotle serve meat that's nearly entirely raised without any antibiotics. Chick-fil-A (which serves almost exclusively chicken, mind you) earned an A grade in 2018 as well.

Availability of whole-grain options. Why does this one get special attention? Because of how overly reliant the restaurant and food-service industry is on refined carbs—white bread in bread baskets, white flour in desserts, white potatoes in every form imaginable (mashed, fried, waffled, wedged, and tater-totted). It's the same reason the availability of plant-based entrées gets its own treatment in the final essay in this book—with the status quo being so heavily weighted on the stuff that's bad for us and the planet, NGOs and the like have to go to the trouble of assembling lists of places that offer the better options. Not in a nanny-state kind of way, but in the name of choice: increasing the chance of consumers choosing healthier and more sustainable menu items by having them on the menu to begin with.

Things have improved dramatically in recent years with respect to whole-grain menu options, thanks in no small part to the popularity of customizable bowls—intact whole grains like farro, quinoa, and brown rice are now common bases to choose from. In addition, based on my own tracking as a whole-grains hunter, it's become easier to find at least one whole-wheat bread choice at a deli or sandwich joint, and more oatmeal

3 TIPS FOR EATING HEALTHY AT A FAST FOOD JOINT

1 STRIVE FOR HEALTHY SIDES. The default side with your order might be chips or fries or breakfast potatoes, but ask if you can swap it for a side salad or fruit.

2 DON'T BREAK THE BANK. Rather than going all in on the burger + fries + shake, pick one indulgent item that matters most in your meal. If you really want to treat yourself to a shake, pair it with the healthier grilled chicken sandwich and side salad, for instance. If it's the burger you're craving most, round out your meal with an apple and water.

3 PATROL THE PORTION. Can you do a half-sandwich, half-salad combo? Does the restaurant offer a child-sized entrée? (Sounds silly, but seriously: unnecessary stomachaches! Excessive food waste!) Maybe your order comes with a large soda—can you trade down to a small or choose water instead?

options have appeared on fast food breakfast menus. But still, we have a long way to go. To help you feel less like a salmon swimming upstream, the Whole Grains Council's "Eating Away from Home" page is full of helpful leads. It provides examples of food-service leaders in terms of their whole-grain offerings, including workplace and hospital cafeterias, chain restaurants (along with a special logo for kid-friendly whole-grain choices), and independent restaurants.

Medium to large chain restaurants that get kudos from the Whole Grains Council include Au Bon Pain, Baja Fresh, Bob Evans, Caribou Coffee, Chipotle, Cracker Barrel, Dunkin' Donuts, Pita Pit, Seasons 52, Starbucks, and Zoë's Kitchen.

55

ON BECOMING A HUMANE SOCIETY

The second lens we explore for making food choices away from home is the extent to which a restaurant or food-service operation takes care of the animals in its supply chain and the workers on its front lines.

ANIMALS

By now, many (if not most) fast food and fast casual chains have gone cage-free with their eggs, but the welfare of animals raised for food is still a major sticking point. I'm talking primarily about broiler chickens for direct consumption, pork, and beef. For broiler chickens, a coalition of animal rights groups has called for slower-growing breeds of chickens, more room for them to move around, and better lighting. What happens when birds take longer to grow? They're better off because their breasts are no longer so enlarged that their legs can't support their own weight. Unfortunately, though, the environmental impact (land, water, fertilizer) is actually higher for slower-growing breeds because they require more feed. And it costs growers more, which they often pass on to retailers and consumers. This all goes to the aforementioned philosophy of meat eating: "First, less. Then, better." If we all start eating less chicken, this higher cost won't be so much of an issue.

As of 2019, well over 100 food companies, including dozens of major chain restaurants and large food-service operations, have signed on to the coalition's animal welfare commitments

CHICKENS HAVE GOTTEN BIGGER OVER TIME

Here are the numbers, according to the National Chicken Council.

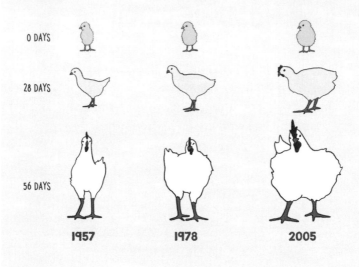

0 DAYS

28 DAYS

56 DAYS

1957   1978   2005

for broiler chickens—from Compass Group and Aramark, the earliest adopters, to Au Bon Pain, Burger King, Chipotle, Jack in the Box, Pret A Manger, Red Robin, Sodexo, Starbucks, and Subway, as well as Royal Caribbean Cruises, Blue Apron, sweetgreen, and Pollo Tropical more recently. The compliance date for nearly all of them is 2024. But no chain has a greater influence on the marketplace than McDonald's. This is because of its sheer size. Unfortunately, it sets its own animal welfare policy, which the coalition considers less ambitious.

Similarly, more than 200 large food companies—McDonald's, IHOP, and Cheesecake Factory, as well as some of the same ones that are on board with the broiler chicken policies, like Aramark, Compass Group, Jack in the Box,

Sodexo, Starbucks, and Subway—have made public commitments vowing to ensure by the year 2022 that the pork they buy does not come from pigs raised in gestation crates. Some chains, like Panera and Chipotle, are already 100 percent gestation-crate-free.

Before you eat at a chain restaurant or large food-service company, check how it fares with respect to these issues of cage-free eggs, chickens that are slower growing and have more space and better lighting, and gestation-crate-free pigs. The following websites track companies' progress toward reaching their commitments on specific animal welfare policies:

* Cage-free eggs: *ciwf.com/eggtrack*
* Animal welfare standards for broiler chickens: *welfarecommitments.com/broiler*
* "Gestation crates food company policies": Entering this search will bring you to a summary of major food companies' commitments to eliminate gestation crates for pigs.

WORKERS

The person behind the register at the average fast food joint is most likely barely scraping by. Minimum wage is the norm, and employer-provided health insurance is a luxury benefit enjoyed by only a minority of these workers. One in seven workers in America works in food in some capacity—from farms to processing to distribution to retail or food service. In the words of the Food Chain Workers Alliance, these people are "the hands that feed us." According to Diners United, the consumer arm of the advocacy group Restaurant Opportunities Centers (ROC) United, an estimated 14 million people work in the restaurant industry as a whole, and nearly 4 million work in fast food alone. They face many challenges in this line of work, like wage theft, fewer hours than they might like (part-time status

THE TIPPING QUESTION

$2.13. That's the federal minimum wage for an employee who earns tips. Technically, employers are required to ensure that tips add up to at least the minimum wage. In practice, this doesn't always happen. As a result, many tipped workers live in poverty. They rely on food stamps and often can't cover their basic needs, much less afford to eat the food they're serving us.

Then there's the deeply unsettling finding from a Cornell University study that both black and white diners tip black restaurant servers less than they tip white servers. Between the wage disparities among restaurant staff, the unpredictability of one's income when relying on tips, and the racial bias, some restaurateurs have done away with tipping altogether. You may see a note on the menu or receipt saying that, in lieu of expecting a tip from you, employees are paid a livable salary and/or offered health insurance or other benefits. This usually means a surcharge on your bill or higher menu prices. Unfortunately, these restaurateurs often wind up going back to tipping, because too many American diners aren't ready to embrace the new model. Perhaps they dislike losing the power to reward or punish service quality, and/or they bristle at what feels like higher costs. In reality, the surcharge is usually well under 20 percent, so the total meal costs the same as it would have with a tip—or even less.

Our psychological barrier to supporting a more equitable compensation system for restaurant workers is troubling for at least two reasons. First, the United States is an outlier in putting the onus of ensuring a livable wage on customers. The restaurateurs who try the "service included" model have often been trying to help us catch up with the rest of the world. Second, when restaurants get rid of tipping, sexual harassment goes down. Because although it's no excuse for untoward behavior from diners, when a female server no longer feels the need to wear revealing clothing or be flirtatious just to ensure a roof over her head, the power dynamic shifts.

exempts employers from having to provide benefits), and unreliable scheduling that makes it difficult to line up child care, schedule additional part-time work, or take classes.

As of this printing, the federal minimum wage is $7.25 an hour. Twenty-nine states and the District of Columbia have instituted higher minimum wages than that, and dozens of local municipalities have gone well beyond both state and federal thresholds. San Francisco became the first US city to achieve the $15 minimum wage across the board, and Seattle's increased minimum wage will be in place by 2021. New York State has been phasing in a $15 minimum wage across the state, though it excludes tipped food-service workers. If you live in a place where regulation has mostly taken care of the issue of ensuring a fair, livable wage for restaurant workers, that simplifies things for you. If not, some restaurants have proactively upped their pay, and you can find the ones in your area by downloading the ROC National Diners' Guide, an app for your phone that lists restaurants considered "High Road" establishments. The criteria for that designation are employers offering higher wages—which should vary based on their role as tipped or untipped workers—as well as benefits like paid sick days (so sick workers stay home rather than spreading their germs to customers), work environments free of sexual harassment, and equitable opportunities to move up the ladder.

56

WHEN NUTRITION GETS PERSONAL

I t's a perfect day for ice cream. My friends and I, party of five, meet up in Seattle at the contemporary version of an ice-cream parlor: vegan and gluten free. We step in, ready to order. Or so we think.

"Hi, ladies! Welcome! Any allergies in the group today? Any dietary no-nos we should know about?" The next fifteen minutes are a blur of questions, qualifiers, and indecision. We are two vegetarians, one allergic to tree nuts, and two eaters (myself included) with no constraints. But even being restriction-free doesn't help in my case, as I try to understand the options: "Are you sure 'activated charcoal' is safe for human consumption? Are those pine needles in that flavor? What does 'soy-free earth balance' mean?" The counter girl ends up calling in reinforcements. We are holding up the line.

It turns out that this particular vegan ice cream establishment relies on cashew milk as its primary substitute for cream. That means our friend with the tree-nut allergy is left with limited options. As soon as we're all served and settled in, we want to try each other's flavors. But we stop our compostable spoons mid-swoop. How many college grads does it take to figure out the licking sequence to spare the allergic friend? Quite a few, as it turns out. It's almost comical. Except I really feel for her.

I'm guessing that at least a milder version of this scene resonates with experiences you've had interacting with waiters and groups of people eating out. From chefs and retailers to tech entrepreneurs and consumer behavior experts, many will tell you that this is what the future of food is all about. A one-size-fits-all approach to food and food-service experiences doesn't work anymore. Which, intuitively, makes sense. Instead, we are shifting to "personalized nutrition," enabling each of us to discover our own optimal diet and avoid foods that could harm us.

It used to be that most people could eat anything, and a few people could eat anything except a few things. Now it seems almost everyone can't or won't eat some things. Though the two categories of people—those who can't and those who won't—are related, they often get conflated. In reality, they're critically different. See the next essay for an understanding of the food allergy epidemic and how to be an empathetic eater toward those who suffer from it.

Many who *choose* not to eat certain foods, though, have taken their elimination diets pretty far. That's my own observation, but you can tell, too, because business is booming: The overall "free from" category has risen to $32 billion, which is nearly the size of the entire organic industry, according to Euromonitor. (The entire packaged foods market, for context, is about $2 trillion.) Gluten-free specifically has gone from a $1.7 billion retail market in 2011 to a projected $4.7 billion in 2020, also according to Euromonitor. Not to mention, restaurant menus have come to look like Egyptian ciphers: GF for "gluten-free," V for "vegan," DF for "dairy-free," and so on.

What's driving the rise of food tribes? As I support in this book, some folks become part of food tribes such as vegan or vegetarian not with the goal of personalizing their nutrition but rather to express various social or environmental values through their eating identities. The many stripes of elimination dieters are to me a different lot, though, and for them, several factors appear to be at play. One is our food culture having become one of fear. Fear of fatness has long been around, but today we've added fear of inflammation and irritation, and a general overtone of avoidance. Diet books, blogs, and multistep miracle programs sell fear to their advantage. Then there's the dramatic social, environmental, and political upheaval we're all navigating. Which brings us to a second potential driver: control. There's great power in saying no. In saying, *I know my body best.* Rather than diets long centered on weight-loss goals, the modern era of aversion is usually about optimizing your own well-being—whatever that means *for you.* Eczema, joint pain, bloating, brain fog, low energy, you name it. More and more people feel that self-experimentation—through food—is the path to healing.

All of this is completely understandable. But our new normal brings a seesaw: What goes down when individualized eating goes up? At least three things, by my count.

For starters, happiness. Countless people shutting out delicious foods in the name of health are robbing themselves of joy. (Again, I'm not talking about people who make food choices based on medical necessity or environmental or human rights issues.) Joy is of course hard to measure, but less of it likely means shorter tempers and less kindness, more tension and more stress—a serious detriment not only to individuals and home lives but communities and workplaces. In other words, if you have a bunch of individual people who are each miserable from all the pleasures they've expelled from their lives, collectively it makes for a pretty miserable society.

Second, diet quality can suffer. People on gluten-free diets are even less likely than gluten eaters to get the recommended amount of whole grains; paleo adherents tend to consume unhealthy levels of red meat; Whole 30 followers are missing out on the benefits of various vegetables and legumes.

Third, commensality. That is, the deeply human experience of breaking bread together. This last caution about food aversions is the potential increase in eating alone. Copious research shows that Americans are already in dire straits in terms of widespread loss of social ties, and personalized nutrition doesn't help the situation. Each of us fixated on our individual litany of banishments makes it awfully hard to convene over something as simple as a lunch date or convivial cocktail. In fact, a 2019 survey found that nearly half of Americans following an exclusion diet of some kind admit it impairs their social life. So, although personalized nutrition makes a lot of sense, keep in mind this potential irony: Despite going down these roads of rejection in the search for long-term well-being, one of the greatest predictors of longevity is actually social connectedness. Rather than focusing on optimizing our unique macronutrient ratios, we'll likely live longer by embracing food as a social act.

57

ETHICAL EATING IN THE ERA OF FOOD ALLERGIES

Odds are you either have a food allergy or have a friend or family member who does.

This is not a niche issue. This is a monumental societal and cultural issue that affects everyone who eats, which is to say: everyone. And it especially affects people in positions like schoolteachers, administrators, and airline stewards, as well as restaurateurs, food product manufacturers, and farmers.

As to why food allergies have risen, theories abound. Children born outside the United States are less likely to have an allergy, and the chance of having one increases after living in the United States for just ten years. Potential problems with Western lifestyles range from the so-called "hygiene hypothesis" and gene-environment interactions that make the body attack itself to the excessive use of antibiotics and questions about what babies are exposed to in utero and how they're delivered. It appears that diet and certain activities early in life—such as spending time outdoors and being breastfed—may help protect against the risk of allergies.

WHAT HAS THE FOOD ALLERGY EPIDEMIC—AND THE RELATED BUT DIFFERENT STRAND OF INCREASED INGREDIENT INTOLERANCE AND FOOD INDIVIDUALISM—MEANT FOR THE ACT OF EATING AWAY FROM HOME?

Cross-contamination and the potential liability risks are taken seriously. May 2016 marked "the first time in Britain that someone has been convicted of manslaughter over the sale of food," according to the *New York Times*. After a peanut-allergic customer

CONSIDER THESE SOBERING STATISTICS:

* The number of health insurance claims from severe reactions caused by food allergies jumped almost 400 percent between 2007 and 2016.

* Roughly $25 billion is spent annually in response to severe allergic reactions to food.

* Food allergies affect children the most—8 percent have at least one, and milk is the most common. About 5 percent of US adults have a food allergy, and shellfish is the most common. (Most children with milk allergy outgrow it.)

* The rate of people with food allergies is doubling roughly every decade. In the 1980s, it was estimated that only 1 percent or less of the population had a food allergy.

died from eating at an Indian restaurant, the owner was said to have a "cavalier" attitude and was sentenced to six years in jail. The *Times* reported, "He had cut corners . . . replacing almond powder in his recipes . . . with a cheaper mix of groundnuts, and hiring untrained, undocumented workers to turn out the popular curry dishes at his restaurants." The silver lining of tragedies like this one is that, over the years, restaurants have beefed up their food safety protocols and staff trainings.

It's changed what's on the menu in the first place. As mentioned, the eight most common allergenic foods in America are crustacean shellfish, eggs, fish, cow's milk, peanuts, soy, tree nuts, and wheat. They account for about 90 percent of food allergies. More and more, rather than finding ways to accommodate individual substitutions, many professional kitchens are doing away with the top eight altogether. Sure, it means the 95 percent of adults with no food allergies aren't eating ingredients there that they might enjoy, but they have countless other opportunities to do so. Frankly, this protocol is easier on restaurant staff and much safer for customers.

As part of my fascination with the rise of food allergies in America, I wrote an article for the *Washington Post* in which I aimed to uncover the ways in which the afflictions of the minority were shaping the food choices available to the majority. I did this in the interest of raising awareness. However, the reader reactions I received made sound points and persuaded me to change my tune. This only continued once I visited an allergy research clinic and started talking to researchers, subscribing to newsletters, watching webinars from allergy awareness advocates, and interviewing parents.

My conversion was part ethical, part empathetic: For one, it was reframed to me as a hidden disability, and wouldn't I support menus made to accommodate food-allergic diners the same way I would support ramps and wide doors for people with wheelchairs? Obviously, yes. Second, parents shared gut-wrenching stories about their families' experiences: watching their toddlers go into anaphylactic shock from a single peanut butter pretzel or lick of cake batter; the burden of constantly remembering to bring their own food to birthday parties and potlucks; the pain of injecting a child with an EpiPen amid the panic of a reaction; the anxiety that the tiniest oversight could mean a trip to the ER; vacations avoided because the destination's nearest hospital didn't have an allergy department; time missed at school by kids, time off required by parents, and far too much time endured in traffic—all to participate in immune therapy treatments and clinical trials; and, on the bright side, for some of those whose treatments were successful, of the enormous weight lifted by moments like the first Halloween they let their children eat regular candy bars without fear of cross-contamination.

So, my message to you is this: Don't be like I was and dismiss allergy-tailored menus as merely catering to fad dieters. It's the choice between one diner's inconvenience and another person's life. And, of course, the people dealing with allergies don't like it either. They'd rather eat birthday cake and PB&Js and not carry an EpiPen around in their pocket. You're a conscious eater, so cut them some slack and help keep them safe.

ALLERGY FYIs

* Whether you're food allergic, the parent of someone who's allergic, or the person picking a restaurant on behalf of a group, check ahead of time to see who in your party might have any food allergies. That way you can avoid a bad experience once you arrive. (For example, if you learn that one person has a peanut allergy, you might not pick the Thai restaurant.) For a nationwide list of restaurants that are particularly friendly to food-allergic diners, consult the AllergyEats guide online: *allergyeats.com.*

* If you or a family member has a serious food allergy, you probably already know that sometimes restaurateurs fail to disclose all the correct information. Follow your intuition if things seem sketchy, and keep medication on you at all times. For gluten and peanut allergies, you might also consider investing in a portable sensor like Nima, which can detect small amounts of gluten and peanut.

* If you don't have a food allergy but have another type of allergy, be aware of "oral allergy syndrome." This is when a non-food allergy leads to an allergic reaction to certain foods. For example, people allergic to birch tree pollen may react to similar proteins found in fruits like peaches, apples, and cherries.

58

THE CASE FOR CALORIE LABELING

After nearly a decade of hullabaloo among legislators and lobbyists, consumer rights advocates and nutritionists, calorie labeling is now the law of the land in the United States—at least for chain restaurants, movie theaters, and other places like convenience stores and vending machines that have twenty or more outlets. Research shows that when eating out compared with at home, we're more likely to overeat, consume less nutritious food, and misjudge calorie content. No question: All of these realities gradually and collectively contribute to the Mayday-level obesity situation we're in—and to the many diet-related chronic diseases that come with it, from high blood pressure to type 2 diabetes.

The unfortunate news is that putting calorie counts on menus only sort of helps. And not everyone, not by that much, not all the time.

That said, with the severity of the health crisis upon us, *any* measure found to help *some* people make *some* positive dent can be quite valuable. For instance, in one study in New York City, only 15 percent of fast food customers used menu labels at all. But those who did ordered about 100 fewer calories for their fast food lunch meal. Which is huge, because the Center for Science in the Public Interest tells us that the whole enchilada of the obesity epidemic is made up of a 200-calorie surplus per person per day (on average). The people in the New York City study would be halfway there.

The *quality* of the snack or meal or beverage you're purchasing is ultimately the most important health consideration related to calories—what it offers by way of nutrients, taste, experience, happiness, provenance, production profile, and so on, and what it costs, so to speak, in terms of any negative nutritional or environmental impact. *But the quantity still matters.*

There are at least three other important reasons that calorie labeling can be worthwhile:

TRANSPARENCY

If nothing else, think of calorie labeling as one window for understanding the food you're about to put into your body. If you're going to down a Starbucks Peppermint Mocha Frappuccino at 450 calories, menu labeling allows you to consume the calories (and gobs of sugar!) intentionally, rather than finding out about the calories and sugar after the fact—or not at all. And if by then you're not feeling so great, labeling can give you insight into why. Or if you're like me and like to play around with the Starbucks nutrition widget, you can see that just skipping the whipped cream saves you more than 100 calories. I don't even like whipped cream, so skipping it actually improves my overall satisfaction with the drink. Or maybe you're craving a Caramel Macchiato but don't really need the grande. Opting for a tall saves at least 40 calories. It's your right to know what you're putting in your body.

REFORMULATION

Guess what might be the best outcome of calorie labeling? Options become healthier before they even hit the menu board. Knowing that they have to divulge the calorie information can motivate food providers to reformulate. Chain restaurants that have had to comply with the regulation—from fast food to sit-down casual spots—may very well have changed the recipes, portion sizes, or positioning of some menu items. And despite the federal law taking effect only in 2018, you no doubt saw calorie labels at chains like Panera and Noah's Bagels years before, since some operations rolled it out nationally once local or state measures were in place.

LESS FOOD WASTE

Many of us have been told since childhood to finish our meal. The (in)famous "Clean Plate Club." But when we're given more nutrition and calorie information about a meal, some of us might instead eat less. That may sound like *more* food waste, but over the long run, it could add up to less. Food waste reduction has caught on like wildfire across the industry. For instance, many chefs now use kitchen scraps as creative ingredients, and in cafeteria buffet settings like colleges and universities, trays are becoming obsolete in order to nudge customers away from both overeating and wasting. The biggest reason is that wasted food is wasted money—money on ingredients, labor, water, energy, etc. The more precisely restaurateurs and food-service professionals can keep their waste down, the better they manage their budgets. And trust me, margins are tight. Operators want to give you enough to keep you from leaving hungry and disgruntled, and to allow you to feel you've gotten your money's worth, but not have too much left on the plate each time.

When people from other parts of the world visit the United States, they're often horrified by the portion sizes. Consider, for instance, that the largest size of fries that McDonald's offers on the American menu is 11 percent bigger than that on the UK menu. Portion sizes have become at least twice as big and up to eight times as big as a "standard serving size" set by the USDA and FDA. Based on a chart from the *Waste-Free Kitchen Handbook*, between 1982 and 2002, the estimated restaurant portion size doubled for a basic bowl of spaghetti and meat-balls, tripled for a soda, and quintupled for a chocolate chip cookie. All this despite much sensory and psychology research showing that we get the most pleasure from the first few bites of a food, with enjoyment falling off with each subsequent bite. And, that it's the pleasure of the final bite of something that determines the pleasure we feel after eating it. Which means that smaller portions are actually *more* satisfying.

When portions are too large, we eat too much food, waste some of it, or do both.

Bottom line: For a clean conscience and a clean plate, aim for reasonable portions when you eat away from home—by using calorie labeling where it's available, and ordering only what you can eat.

BETWEEN 1982 AND 2002, THE ESTIMATED RESTAURANT PORTION SIZE TRIPLED FOR A SODA AND QUINTUPLED FOR A CHOCOLATE CHIP COOKIE.

1982   2002

59

FARM-TO-TABLE:
THEY'RE NOT ALL HUCKSTERS

When I first saw an exposé in the *Tampa Bay Times* in 2016 uncovering lies and cheating in the farm-to-table business, my heart sank. A rigorous investigation finally proved what many had speculated and others had probably feared but tried to dismiss—that often the local, artisanal, farm-fresh promises touted by quaint restaurants were empty ones: "local" farms that were actually far, far away, or listing a fishmonger on a restaurant's sourcing chalkboard who's never heard of the place. After this scandal about higher-end restaurants, investigations of fast food chains with similar rosily spun stories unearthed much of the same.

The writer of the series of articles, Laura Reiley, summed up the conundrum: "Most restaurants buy food from one of a small handful of distributors who source products in bulk at the best price from around the world [e.g., Sysco and US Foods] . . . Most restaurants do not have the time or wherewithal to deal directly with farmers and producers; most farmers and producers don't have the infrastructure to do their own sales, marketing, and delivery. So the storytelling begins."

Therein lies the problem: We so badly *want* the new wave to be here now. And yet the day-to-day reality of turning a bear of a food system on its head is a Sisyphean task.

On the bright side, many restaurants do what they say they do: establish sourcing relationships with farmers in their region. These afford you, the diner, with not just connection to place but often greater variety, freshness, and flavor.

Hospitals, K–12 schools and entire school districts, corporate employers, and colleges and universities are having an even greater impact in terms of improving food systems. These farm-to-institution relationships provide benefits in several areas: bolstering local economies; serving as a launchpad for food literacy through educational programs, on-site farmers' markets, and field trips for students, employees, and patients; and supporting rural farm communities by giving farmers larger and more reliable incomes. This financial stability can help farmers build savings to invest in better equipment and new technologies. Those tools, in turn, can improve crop yields, land and water use, and their ability to manage risk and resources, all of which can mean better products and better soil health, not to mention more competitive positioning against major agribusiness producers. Farm-to-institution relationships can also give you, the diner, more meaningful and tasty food experiences.

HERE'S A ROUNDUP OF RESOURCES THAT CAN HELP YOU IDENTIFY LEGIT LOCAL SOURCING EFFORTS:

* The Good Food Purchasing Program is an exemplary framework for evaluating an institution's commitment to all the tenets of being a conscious eater. Supporting local economies is, naturally, among their core values. You can search for whether your local school district has adopted the program. Los Angeles Unified School District was the first, and San Francisco Unified, Oakland Unified, Boulder Valley School District, and Chicago Public Schools have all come on board.

* Though not an auditor or third-party verifier, the National Farm to School Network is a resource for understanding what it might mean to choose a school—and therefore a

food-service provider—for your child that is truly championing local agriculture and bringing farm-related educational experiences into the classroom, cafeteria, and school garden.

* A similar, regionally based organization is Farm to Institution New England, whose website you can scour to learn about schools, colleges, and health care organizations (think hospitals and nursing homes) in their network who take local and regional food systems seriously.

* For fine-dining experiences, *Travel + Leisure* compiled an exhaustive list in 2017 of what its editors deem to be the most committed and worth-the-trip farm-to-table restaurant in each of the fifty states plus Washington, DC.

60

EAT LIKE THE PLANET DEPENDS ON IT

Every day, about three times a day, each one of us has the responsibility, and delicious opportunity, to align our food choices with our personal values. Whether you've always thought of food this way, started recently to think of it this way, or only as a result of enjoying my lovely voice in this book have now been persuaded to think of it this way, I can't resist being that food writer who reminds you of this important point. These values might be ones we hold closely, indivisible from our identities and how we see ourselves. Or these values might be more aspirational—those we would like to see more of in the world, and those we wish to embody more as we grow and age and serve as role models for our kids. Wherever the values lie on your personal spectrum of reality versus aspiration, this responsibility and opportunity call us to the adage of "voting with your fork."

When selecting your next restaurant for a gathering of family or friends, date night, or business lunch, or deciding where to order delivery for your kid's birthday party, or choosing a caterer for the bridal shower you're hosting, try to consider not merely the place that's the cheapest or tastiest or healthiest or most convenient (though those are good reasons), but also whether that restaurant is doing its part to address the overwhelming urgency of climate change. To make an environmentally conscious decision about which restaurants to patronize, take the following into account.

OVERALL SUSTAINABILITY

The quickest way to get this information may be from the non-profit Green Restaurant Association. They certify restaurants on a four-star scale across eight environmental indicators: water efficiency, waste reduction and recycling, sustainable durable goods and building materials, sustainable food, energy, reusables and environmentally preferable disposables, chemical and pollution reduction, and transparency and education. The Green Restaurant Association has been assessing restaurants since its founding in 1990. So far, the certification has been earned by independently run coffee shops, cafés, fine-dining restaurants, and select venues in corporate and university settings, rather than large-scale chain restaurants or food-service companies. Search *dinegreen.com* for listings of certified green restaurants by state.

AVAILABILITY OF PLANT-BASED MEALS

Power begins with choice—so finding places to eat where you can choose from a variety of plant-based meals is key to being an empowered conscious eater. Why? Because the status quo is meat-centric menus wherever you go, and we know that plant-based foods tend to have lower water and carbon footprints. Enter the Good Food Restaurant Scorecard. It's an annual ranking of the top 100 restaurant brands in the United States based on the extent of their plant-based menu options. The Good Food Institute rates each company on a ten-point scale based on factors such as:

* entrées that are completely plant-based (no ingredients coming from animals);

* having default entrées be free of meat, meaning a customer might be able to add chicken to a pasta order, but it's been decoupled from the base entrée;

❋ plant-based foods given prominence and positioning or marketing on the menu, i.e., being part of the main menu rather than something available upon request, to normalize plant-based eating.

Jamba Juice and White Castle (yes, you read that right) tied for the top spot in 2018, with scores of 9, and Panera and Yard House were close behind with 8.75 and 8.5, respectively. Others that earned a score of 7 or above included Chipotle, Domino's, Maggiano's, Noodles & Company, Olive Garden, Starbucks, TGI Fridays, and two elevated convenience store chains, Sheetz and Wawa.

SUSTAINABLE SEAFOOD

Since seafood is one of the most complicated things to eat sustainably, consulting Seafood Watch's list of restaurant partners and business partners who champion its standards allows you to make an intelligent choice with minimal effort. You want a spot that does not serve items from the organization's "Avoid" list (indicated by a red color coding on its materials), has trained its staff on sustainable seafood issues, and is committed to selling only seafood that is environmentally responsible.

Seafood Watch business partners and restaurant partners include Aramark, Bamboo Sushi, Bon Appétit Management Company, Border Grill, Brown Bag Seafood, California Fish Grill, Red Lobster, Sodexo, and Whole Foods Market (don't forget the meals you get from "grocerants"—food courts, countertop dining spots, and the like, in grocery stores).

PALM OIL SOURCING

Since palm oil often plays a significant role in professional kitchens, I recommend checking the World Wildlife Fund's Palm Oil Buyers Scorecard for food service as a good way to see who is committed to sourcing from only the most responsible palm oil producers.

As of the latest analysis (2016), the food-service companies leading the pack were Krispy Kreme Doughnuts, McDonald's, Sodexo, and Restaurant Brands International, which owns Burger King, Popeyes, and Tim Hortons. They all received a score of 9 out of 9 for sustainable palm oil sourcing.

CARBON FOOTPRINT

A new category of sustainable restaurants is emerging around carbon neutrality. These restaurants carefully track their carbon emissions and employ eco-friendly practices and carbon offset projects to bring their total down to zero. Carbon can be a useful metric for the overall sustainability of a restaurant because it's simple and widely understood. Companies in various industries have carbon neutrality programs they're committed to, or that they offer customers. The entire state of California is trying to reach carbon-neutral status by the year 2045. As we've discussed, a carbon footprint doesn't cover *everything* related to sustainability (water is still mega-important, for example), but it does check quite a few boxes—from food waste and energy use to healthy soil and animal agriculture.

Certified by a nonprofit called ZeroFoodprint, some restaurants have gone carbon-neutral year-round, like world-renowned noma in Copenhagen and benu in San Francisco. Hundreds more across the globe—from Fort Wayne, Indiana, and Nashville, Tennessee, to New York City and Shanghai—have gone carbon-neutral on Earth Day in recent years. You can imagine being able to search OpenTable or Yelp by a "sustainable restaurant" or "carbon-neutral restaurant" filter. For now, check *zerofoodprint.org* for the complete list. New restaurants are coming on board all the time, and soon enough the status won't be confined to the fine-dining, break-the-bank type of places.

THE CHEF'S ROLE

Whether we think it's a good thing or not, chefs hold tremendous influence in our culture. Through their celebrity status, big personalities, huge social media followings, vast product lines, cookbooks, and ubiquity online and on TV, they help shape our perceptions of how things are, or should be, in society. Case in point: Chef José Andrés, of Washington, DC, and his nomination for the 2019 Nobel Peace Prize. (He did Herculean humanitarian work feeding millions of Hurricane Maria survivors in Puerto Rico.)

It's not just celebrity chefs who are levers for changing norms in our culture, though. The fact that the food industry overall is one of the largest employers in our country, coupled with the fact that everybody eats, creates a situation where the experience we have at a restaurant—the things we learn there, the ways it expands our minds and palates, even sub-consciously, all of it—can be a powerful vehicle for change. In recent years, we've seen this potential realized by female chefs and restaurant workers helping propel the #MeToo movement forward and speaking up for women's rights more broadly, as well as fast food workers leading the nation-wide charge for a $15 minimum wage. In my mind, climate change is the issue whose time has come to be mainstreamed through food.

If enough people gradually and cumulatively vote with not just their forks but their grocery baskets, we may very well be headed for a revolution. One in which *gastronomic citizenship* becomes the norm. A day when you no longer need a guide to conscious eating—because it will be so second nature, we'll just call it . . . eating.

TOP 5 TAKEAWAYS

1 Healthy fast food is not necessarily an oxymoron, but a dose of skepticism and a little research ahead of time will help.

2 Patronize restaurants with sustainable operations, local and regional sourcing, and humane treatment of animals and workers. Consult online resources from consumer watchdog groups and NGOs.

3 Help yourself and the planet by using calorie labels and judicious ordering. Many portions are enough for two.

4 Check company websites and third-party guides to support restaurateurs who treat their workers with dignity and fair pay.

5 Consumer demand has driven most of the progress for eliminating antibiotics and improving animal welfare in the meat supply. Consult the Consumer Reports antibiotic scorecards and online trackers of restaurant companies' animal welfare policies to find the most responsible operators—and keep up the pressure on the rest of them.

10 SOURCES I TRUST

When you have a question I haven't answered, here are ten sources to consult. I'm confident they would tackle the topic with evidence-based reasoning and clear explanations.

1 BERKELEY WELLNESS, *berkeleywellness.com*

2 CONSUMER REPORTS, *consumerreports.org*

3 *EATINGWELL* MAGAZINE, *eatingwell.com*

4 ENVIRONMENTAL WORKING GROUP, *ewg.org*

5 HARVARD T. H. CHAN SCHOOL OF PUBLIC HEALTH'S NUTRITION SOURCE, *hsph.harvard.edu/nutritionsource*

6 MAYO CLINIC, *mayoclinic.org*

7 THE *NEW YORK TIMES* WELL SECTION, *nytimes.com/well*

8 OLDWAYS WHOLE GRAINS COUNCIL, *wholegrainscouncil.org*

9 WEBMD, *webmd.com*

10 WORLD RESOURCES INSTITUTE, *wri.org*

GLOSSARY

Select acronyms and key terms whose meanings are easy to mix up or forget

AICR: American Institute for Cancer Research

BPA: Bisphenol A, a harmful industrial chemical found in many single-use plastics, the lining of some canned goods, and store register receipts, among other things

CAFOs: Confined animal feeding operations

Carbon footprint: In this context, the amount of greenhouse gases (GHG), especially carbon dioxide, emitted to grow, process, and deliver a food product to us

CDC: Centers for Disease Control and Prevention

EPA: US Environmental Protection Agency

FDA: US Food and Drug Administration

Gut microbiome: The community of microbes that inhabits each of our intestinal tracts

HCAs: Heterocyclic amines, potentially carcinogenic compounds generated from grilling (the char on grilled meat)

HDL cholesterol: "Good" cholesterol

HFCs: Hydrofluorocarbons, the chemicals that chill refrigerators and air conditioners and are powerful contributors to global warming

LDL cholesterol: "Bad" cholesterol

Monounsaturated fat: Liquid at room temperature, it lowers LDL and can raise HDL in certain cases. For a healthy diet, make most of the fat consumed monounsaturated, along with polyunsaturated fat.

Neonics: Short for neonicotinoids, a type of pesticide that is meant to kill pests but also harms honeybees

NSF International: An organization that helps consumers with issues related to the health and safety of food, water, and various products

Omega-3: Omega-3 fatty acids, a type of healthy polyunsaturated fat, of which you want at least a serving a day

Organic: Essentially means no synthetic pesticides, no growth hormones, and no antibiotics were used in the production of the food item

PAHs: Polycyclic aromatic hydrocarbons, potentially carcinogenic compounds generated from grilling (they can coat grilled food through the smoke)

PCBs: Polychlorinated biphenyls, toxic chemicals found in some fish (especially farmed salmon) because of contaminated waters that fish inhabit

Percent Daily Value: The Daily Value is how much of a given nutrient you should either aim to reach or keep below. Knowing how much—the percent—of that amount is in a given food can help you keep track.

Phthalates: Endocrine disruptors that interfere with the normal functioning of hormones in the body; found in some plastics

Polyunsaturated fat: Have essentially the same health effects as monounsaturated fat; also liquid at room temperature. Polyunsaturated fat gets special points for omega-3s, which have other health-promoting properties like keeping heart rates steady. This is useful in preventing death from heart disease and offers benefits to the immune system and brain function, not to mention eyesight and conditions like eczema.

Prebiotics: Found in fruits, vegetables, whole grains, nuts, beans, and seeds, they're plant fibers that are the key food source for your gut bacteria. Because they help microbes grow, prebiotics have been likened to fertilizers for your gut.

Probiotics: Strains of bacteria, living organisms, that you add to the current residents in your gut when you eat foods that contain them

Saturated fat: Solid at room temperature, saturated fat raises bad cholesterol (LDL) *and* good cholesterol (HDL), but high intake overall is associated with higher risk of heart disease

Trans fat: A type of fat that was recently banned in the US but has historically been in our food supply as the artificial form of partially hydrogenated oils. Typically solid at room temperature, it raises bad cholesterol (LDL) and promotes blood clot formation, which can lead to heart attacks and strokes. Trans fat is also tied to insulin resistance—a precursor to diabetes—and a host of other health issues.

USDA: US Department of Agriculture

Water footprint: In this context, the amount of water used to grow, process, and deliver a food product to us

WHO: World Health Organization

ACKNOWLEDGMENTS

Foremost thanks go to my agent, Danielle Svetcov, of Levine | Greenberg | Rostan, whose creativity, persistence, and wisdom made this book possible. Thank you for your premium blend of straight talk and pep talk—and for being the brilliant advisor I'd been looking for all this time.

I'm grateful for the sharp eyes and great ideas of Amy Gash, Suzie Bolotin, Mary Ellen O'Neill, Rae Ann Spitzenberger, Hillary Leary, and everyone at Workman who touched the book. Mary Ellen, your tree-trimming made my pages pop, and I simply adore working together.

Sincere gratitude—and admiration—to Iris Gottlieb, the talented illustrator with whom we collaborated in order to bring the vision for this book to life.

Courtney Quirin provided far more than fact-checking—and killer FC at that—but went above the call of duty to serve as a real research partner. Thank you for your diligence and passion for the project.

My stable of early readers helped me take my mountain of clay and sculpt it into an actionable final product. Thank you for your invaluable feedback: Ali Kelley, Annie Grevers, Ashley Clave, Caitlin Eck, Dr. Cristin Young, Erin Weekley, Kristen Rasmussen de Vasquez, Lisa Davie, Sally Egan, and Sally Rogers.

I owe much appreciation to many individuals who motivate me, but in particular to the following friends and colleagues for supporting this book and my work as an author overall: Dr. Anne McBride, Dara Silverstein, Matt Rothe, Dr. Maureen Timmons, Michael Pollan, and Will Rosenzweig. You fill me up, build me up, and stretch my mind.

Toby Bilanow at the *New York Times*: Thank you for the years of friendship and opportunity. Not to mention, the exceptional editing you provide time and again. Our work together on AskWell articles, answering readers' most burning questions about food and health, has been a major driver behind this book.

I'm thankful for my parents, Joni Balter and Tim Egan, for nourishing me now as ever. You've done so both literally—through more delicious, adventurous meals than I can count—and professionally, through your own careers and active encouragement of my itch to make books. You inspire me every day.

Finally, to my husband, Sam Kintz. Thank you for continuing to be what you've always been: my sounding board, my biggest fan, and my best friend. You're my deepest reservoir of energy and resilience. I love that you believe I could write a masterpiece while sitting in "the dusty corner between an industrial refrigerator and a storage closet on an upside-down milk crate with a flickering fluorescent light." I've said it before and I'll say it again: One day our boys will discover there's more than one writer in the house.

INDEX

A

Acesulfame potassium, 199, 200, 205
Agave nectar, 196, 198, 204
Alcohol, 137, 140, 141, 161
Allergies, 7, 28, 53, 55, 86, 106, 186, 209–10, 236, 237, 240–43
Almond(s), 4–7, 84, 89; milk, 48, 49, 51
Aloe vera, 204
Aluminum cans, 165–66
American Grassfed, 52, 98, 102, 132, 149, 150–51
Anchovies, 104, 105, 115, 116
Animal-based foods, 81–157; antibiotics in production of, 129–33 (see also antibiotics); conscious carnivore and, 92–99; feed conversion efficiency of, 192–93; fraud and, 85–88; Great Protein Myth and, 89–91; lighter footprint of plant food vs., 83; processed meat and cancer, 134–38; raw, safe handling of, 132; third-party certification labels for, 98, 99, 101–2, 111, 112, 119, 125–27, 132–33, 146–56, 157. *See also specific foods*
Animal welfare, 94, 96–99, 147–49; eggs and, 124, 125–26, 127; Five Freedoms for, 96; restaurant policies and, 133, 231–33, 257
Animal Welfare Approved, 52, 98, 125–26, 132, 147, 148, 154

Antibiotics, 53, 93, 97–98, 240; farmed fish and, 113, 116; grass-fed animals and, 52, 100, 150; in restaurants' meat supply, 133, 227–28, 257; superbugs and resistance to, 129–33; third-party certification and, 75, 98, 126, 132–33, 146, 149–50, 155
Apples, 6, 18, 19, 42, 43, 55
Aquaculture Stewardship Council (ASC), 112, 119, 153–54
Arsenic, 39–41, 212
Ascorbic acid, 203
Aspartame, 200, 205

B

Bacon, 94, 123, 134, 136–37, 138
Bananas, 18, 43, 50, 54, 76, 208
B Corporations, 35
Beans. See Legumes
Beef, 3, 23–25, 27, 28, 45, 47, 82, 83, 84, 86, 94, 95, 97, 132, 192, 193, 231; antibiotics and, 52, 100, 150, 227–28; grass-fed, 47, 52, 98, 100–2, 150–51; processed meats, 134–38
Beverage bottles, 8–12, 164–66, 172
BHA, 205
Biodiversity, 74, 77, 78
Biodynamic, 21, 71, 78
Bird Friendly, 77
Blockchain, 87
Blood sugar, 33, 42, 43, 53, 169, 180, 187, 190, 198, 204, 212
BPA, 166, 169–70, 172
Bran, 29, 30, 32, 188

Breastfeeding, 140
Bulk, buying in, 162, 164, 172, 175
Butter, 45, 46, 47, 64, 162

C

Caffeine, 205
Calories, 176, 189–95, 221;
    contribution to overall health
    and, 189–90, 194; empty, 191,
    194; labeling and, 244–47
Cancer risk, 15, 39, 48, 50, 134–45,
    169, 204, 213; added sugar and,
    198–99; artificial sweeteners
    and, 200, 205; chemicals and,
    17, 72, 114, 185; grilling and,
    142–45; lifestyle choices and,
    139–41; meat and, 91, 134–38,
    142–45
Canned foods, 161, 165–66, 172
Canola oil, 62, 63, 64–65
Caramel coloring, 204
Carbohydrates, 33, 176, 180
Carbon farming, 74
Carbon footprint, 7, 22, 83, 116,
    166, 217, 252, 254–55, 259
Carbon neutrality, 254–55
Cellulose, 85–86, 87, 204
Certified Humane Raised and
    Handled, 52, 98, 126, 132, 148,
    154
Cheese, 3, 6, 25, 46, 48, 59, 84,
    122, 208; cellulose as filler in,
    85 86, 87, 204
Chefs, role of, 255–56
Chickens, 6, 47, 52, 82, 94, 97,
    98, 104, 127, 138, 227, 228;
    antibiotics and, 126, 130–33,
    149, 155; cage-free, 97, 98, 126,
    127, 155, 231, 233; free-range
    or free-roaming, 126, 127, 154,
    155–56; humane treatment
    of, 96–98, 125–26, 148, 231–33;
    omega-3s label, 156; pasture-
    raised, 126, 127, 155, 156;
    vegetarian fed, 126, 127–28,
    156. See also Eggs
Children, young, produce for, 11,
    16, 19, 40, 53, 105, 114, 169, 240

Cholesterol, 121–23, 180
Citric acid, 203
Coconut: milk, 49; oil, 66–67
Coffee, 6, 77, 87, 173, 205
Community-supported
    agriculture (CSA), 88
Compost, 72, 73
Confined animal feeding
    operations (CAFOs), 92, 93,
    97–98, 100, 113
Consumer demand, 195
Corn oil, 64
Crop rotation and cover crops,
    72, 73

D

Dairy products, 27, 84, 101, 206–7;
    grass-fed, 52, 101, 102. See also
    specific foods
Dates on labels, 183, 206–8
Diabetes, 33, 42, 123, 198, 213
Dietary supplements, 55
Diet soda, 190, 194
Diversification of food we eat, 20
Diversified farms, 99

E

Eggs, 3, 6, 27, 94, 97, 98, 104,
    121–28, 208, 209, 210, 231,
    241; brown vs. white, 124;
    cage-free, 97, 98, 126, 127,
    155, 231, 233; cartons for,
    128; cholesterol and, 121–23;
    labels of, 125–28, 154–56;
    refrigeration of, 124
Endosperm, 29, 30, 188
Environmental Working Group
    (EWG): Consumer Guide to
    Seafood, 110, 111; Dirty Dozen
    and Clean Fifteen, 18, 19
Erosion of soil, 64, 72

F

Fair trade certification, 67, 76–77
Farmers, well-being of, 72–73,
    76–77, 92, 99, 118
Farmers' markets, 73–74, 88
Farm-to-table restaurants, 248–50

Fast food, 224. *See also* Restaurants
Fats, dietary, 45–47, 176–78, 179.
   See also Oils
Feed conversion efficiency, 192–93
Fermented foods, 53–55, 161
Fertilizers, 14, 26, 37, 72
Fiber, dietary, 29–30, 79, 140, 213;
   in fruit, 42, 43; gut microbiome
   and, 53–55, 179; on labels, 179,
   180
Fish and seafood, 3, 27, 47, 82–84,
   103–20, 132, 138, 192, 193,
   209, 241; farmed, 108, 112,
   113–16; foodborne illness from,
   106; fraud and, 86; mercury
   in, 104–6, 110; nutrients in,
   103–4; PCBs in, 114; slavery at
   sea and, 117–20; smoked and
   cured, 134, 136; sustainability
   of, 87–88, 107–12, 253–54;
   third-party certification labels
   and, 111, 119, 151–54. *See also*
   Seafood Watch
Flax milk, 49, 50
Flaxseed oil, 62, 63
Flexitarian diet, 61, 82, 141, 187
Fluoridation, 11
Food dyes, 205
Food fraud, 85–88
Food Justice Certified, 16, 99
Food waste, 22–25, 68, 94, 215,
   217–18, 246–47
Freezing food, 25
Frozen foods, 68–70, 106
Fructose, 42–44
Fruit juice, 43, 44
Fruits, 3, 104, 161, 192, 194, 195,
   199, 201; dried, 43, 44; grilling,
   143–44; sugar in, 42–44. *See
   also* Produce

G

Germ, 29, 30, 32, 41, 188
Glass containers, 165, 166, 167,
   171, 175
Global Animal Partnership (GAP)
   Certified, 98, 126, 133, 149,
   154–55

Gluten avoidance, 187, 211–13,
   237, 238, 243
Goat, 27, 82, 92, 94, 97, 100
Grains, refined and enriched,
   30–31, 188; why people eat,
   32–33
Grains, whole, 29–34, 161, 188,
   195, 213, 228–30; anatomy of,
   29–30, 188; buying local, 35;
   cooking time for, 32–33; intact,
   30; labels of, 34; landrace,
   heirloom, and ancient, 36–37;
   lesser-known options, 35–38;
   milling yourself, 37–38;
   servings of, 30, 31; tips for
   enjoying, 35–38; why people
   don't eat more, 32–33
Grass-fed animals, 47, 52, 98,
   100–2, 150–51
Grilling, cancer risk and, 142–45
Growth hormones, 52, 75, 93, 126,
   146, 149, 150, 155
Gut microbiome, 53–55, 131, 179,
   200

H

Ham, 134
Health halo effect, 184–85
Hemp milk, 48, 49
Herbicides, 17
Herring, 105, 115, 116
Honey, 198
Hot dogs, 134, 136–37, 138, 206–7

I

Illnesses, foodborne, 21, 106,
   206–7
Ingredients, 180, 181, 221; clean-
   label movement and, 160, 162,
   203; safe vs. scary, 203–4

K

Kernza, 74

L

Labels, 176–88, 221; allergies and,
   209–10; clean-label movement
   and, 160, 162, 203; dates on,

183, 206–8; distraction tactics and, 183–85; on front of product, 182–86; health claims on, 183, 186; ingredients on, 160, 162, 180, 181, 203–4, 221; Nutrition Facts panel, 33, 176–80, 181, 183, 185, 221; of whole grains, 34; words with little meaning on, 185–86. *See also* Third-party certification labels

Lactose, 42, 50

Lamb (and sheep), 23, 27, 45, 82, 94, 97, 100

Lead, in drinking water, 9, 11–12

Leftovers, 25, 215, 217–18

Legumes (beans), 26–28, 74, 84, 104, 192, 195

M

Manure, 72

Marine Stewardship Council (MSC), 111, 119, 152–53

Meal kits, 214–20

Meat, 92–102, 122, 210, lab-grown, 94–95; nose-to-tail eating and, 94; processed, 134–38, 206–7. *See also* Animal-based foods; Animal welfare; *specific meats*

Mercury, 86, 104–6, 110, 212

Metabolic syndrome, 198

Microplastics, 168–69

Milks: cow's, 3, 6, 48, 50, 51, 52, 59, 122, 208, 209, 210, 241; plant-based, 48–51

Millet, 36, 37

Modified food starch, 203–4

Mold, 206, 208

Monounsaturated fat, 46

Mulch, 72

Multigrain, 34

N

"Natural," on labels, 186, 204

Nitrogen fixation, beans and, 26–27

Nut(s), 3, 27, 84, 104, 209, 236, 241; butters, 161, 162; milks, 49; tree, allergies to, 7, 209, 236, 241. *See also specific nuts*

Nutrient-poor foods, 189–90, 191, 194

Nutrification, 188

Nutrition Facts panel, 33, 176–80, 181, 183, 185, 221

O

Oat milk, 48–50

Oats and oatmeal, 31–32, 228–30

Ocean pollution, 168–69

Oils, 3, 62–65; coconut, 66–67; palm, 64, 254; production methods and point of origin of, 64–65; smoke point of, 62–63

Olive oil, 62, 63, 65, 66–67, 86, 161

Omega-3 fatty acids, 103–4, 114, 128, 156

Organic foods, 14–17, 19, 71, 73; being strategic on, 18; Certified Organic or USDA Organic, 75–76, 126, 133, 146–47, 155; oils, 65; regenerative agriculture and, 71–74; rice, arsenic in, 40

P

Packaged foods, 159–221; added sugars in, 178–79, 180, 181, 196–202; containers and packaging materials for, 160, 164–66, 214, 215, 216, 217, 219, 221; healthfulness of processed foods and, 161–63; labels of, 176–86 (*see also* Labels); meal kits, 214–20; profits and, 194–95; safe vs. scary ingredients in, 203–4

Palm oil, 64, 163, 254

Paris climate agreement, 90

Parmesan, 85–86, 87, 204

Partially hydrogenated oils, 178

PCBs, 114

PCO Certified 100% Grassfed, 52, 102, 151

Peanut(s): allergies to, 28, 241, 242, 243; butter, 162; oil, 63

Percent Daily Value, 176, 185
Perennial crops, 74
Personalized nutrition, 236–39
Pesticides, 16–17, 18, 64, 75, 113; pollinator protection and, 57–58; washing off residue, 19, 21
Phthalates, 170
Plant-based foods, 79; feed conversion efficiency of, 192; lighter footprint of, 83; third-party certification labels for, 75–78; vegan or vegetarian diet and, 59–61, 157, 218–19, 237. *See also* Fruits; Produce; Vegetables; *specific foods*
Plant-based meals, at restaurants, 228, 252–53
Plastics: bottled water and, 10, 164–65; BPA linings and, 166, 169–70, 172; detriment to ocean health and, 168–70; heat and, 171; packaged foods and, 160, 164; recycling, 10, 128, 165, 168, 173–74, 215; single-use, pros and cons of, 167–70; ten ways to break up with, 171–74
Pollinator protection, 56–58
Polyunsaturated fat, 46–47
Pork (and pigs), 3, 23, 27, 45, 47, 82, 132, 192, 193, 231; humane treatment of, 96–98, 148, 231, 233; processed meats, 134–38
Portion sizes. *See* Serving sizes
Potassium, 185
Poultry, 3, 27, 82–84, 192, 193, 210; antibiotics and, 130–33; processed foods, 134–38. *See also* Chickens; Eggs
Prebiotics and probiotics, 54–55
Pregnant women, 11, 17, 19, 200, 206–7; fish in diet of, 103, 104–6, 114
Processed foods: meats, 134–38, 206–7. *See also* Packaged foods
Produce: best for your health, 13; buying, practical tips for, 18–21; organic, 14–17, 18, 19;

regional eating and, 20–21; seasonal, 19, 79; serving size of, 13; washing, 19, 21. *See also specific foods*
Protein, 179; Great Protein Myth, 89–91; greenhouse gas emissions per gram of, for various foods, 27; health risks of eating too much, 90–91

R

Recycling, 10, 128, 165, 166, 168, 173–74, 215
Red meat, 3, 82, 84, 92; antibiotics and, 130–33; avoiding waste of, 23–25, 94; cancer risk and, 91, 134–38, 142–45; processed, 134–38. *See also specific meats*
"Reduced," on labels, 185–86
Refrigeration, 68–70
Regenerative agriculture, 71
Regional eating, 20–21
Restaurants, 218, 223–57; animal welfare policies of, 133, 231–33, 257; calorie labeling in, 244–47; carbon-neutral, 254–55; categories of, 224–25; farm-to-table, 248–50; food allergies and, 236, 237, 240–43; "healthy" fast food and, 226–30, 257; meal kits vs., 214–15; personalized nutrition and, 236–39; plant-based meals at, 228, 252–53; sustainability issues and, 251–55; tipping in, 234; worker safety and treatment in, 233–35, 256, 257
Rice, 3, 27; arsenic in, 39–41, 212; milk, 49

S

Saccharin, 200, 205
Salmon, 104, 110, 111, 113–14, 116
Salt, 178, 184, 212–13; preserving food with, 134, 135, 136; sea, 204
Sardines, 104, 105, 110, 111

Saturated fat, 45–46, 47, 176–78, 179, 185
School food programs, 249–50
Seafood. *See* Fish and seafood
Seafood Watch, 88, 107–10, 111, 116, 119, 151–52
Seasonal produce, 19, 79
Seeds, 104
Serving (portion) sizes: of fruits and vegetables, 13; on labels, 176; in restaurants, 226, 229, 246–47, 257
Sesame oil, 62, 63
Shopping lists, 23
Shrimp, 117–20
Slavery at sea, 117–20
Soda, 8, 10, 42, 166, 169, 190, 194, 195
Sodium, 178; "reduced," 185–86
Soil health, 71–74
Soy(bean), 27, 60, 209, 241; milk, 48, 49, 50, 51; oil, 47, 64
Straws, 169, 173
Styrofoam, 128, 165
Sugars: added, 178–79, 180, 181, 196–202, 212–13; AHA-recommended Daily Value of, 196; artificial sweeteners and, 199–200; in fruit (fructose), 42–44; many names of, 197; in milk and yogurt (lactose), 42
Sunflower oil, 63, 64, 74
Superbugs, 129–33
Sweeteners: artificial, 190, 199–200, 205. *See also* Sugars

T

Takeout, 218; meal kit vs., 215–16
Teff, 36, 37
Third-party certification labels, 183; for animal-based foods, 98, 99, 101–2, 111, 112, 119, 125–27, 132–33, 146–56, 157; for plant-based foods, 34, 75–78
Tillage, regenerative agriculture and, 73, 74
Tipping, 234
Tocopherol, 204

Tofu, 94
Trans fat, 45, 46, 178, 179
Tuna, 115
Turkey, 82, 94, 132, 135

U

Unsaturated fats, 46–47, 66, 103

V

Vegan and vegetarian diets, 59–61, 157, 218–19, 237
Vegetables, 3, 104, 161, 192, 194, 195, 201; grilling, 143–44. *See also* Produce

W

Walnut oil, 62, 63
Water, 8–12, 195; containers for, 164–66; cost of, 8–9; fizzy, home bubble makers for, 164–65; footprint (of foods) and, 6; safety of, 9, 11–12; sparkling, making your own, 12; from wells, 11, 72
Weight, 8, 42, 136, 139, 140, 198; cancer risk and, 136, 139
Wells, drinking water from, 11, 72
Wheat, 27, 32, 36, 37, 38, 72, 188, 209, 241. *See also* Gluten avoidance
Whole foods, 161–62, 163, 180. *See also* Grains, whole
Whole grains. *See* Grains, whole
Whole Grains Council, 31, 33, 34, 35–36, 230
Workers in the food system and farmers, well-being of, 72–73, 76–77, 92, 99, 118, 233–35, 256, 257

Z

Zero-waste lifestyle, 174

ABOUT THE AUTHOR

SOPHIE EGAN, MPH, is the Director of Health and Sustainability Leadership as well as the Editorial Director for Strategic Initiatives at The Culinary Institute of America. Based in San Francisco, Egan is a contributor to the *New York Times'* Health section, and she has written about food and health for the *Washington Post, EatingWell, Time*, the *Wall Street Journal, Bon Appétit*, WIRED, *Edible San Francisco*, and other publications. Her first book, *Devoured: How What We Eat Defines Who We Are* (William Morrow), is a journey into the American food psyche. Egan holds a master's degree in public health, with a focus on health and social behavior, from the University of California, Berkeley, where she was a Center for Health Leadership fellow. She also holds a bachelor of arts with honors in history from Stanford University. In 2016, she was named one of the UC Global Food Initiative's 30 Under 30. In 2018, she earned a certificate from the Harvard Executive Education in Sustainability Leadership program at the Center for Climate, Health, and the Global Environment. You can find her on Twitter @SophieEganM and at *sophieegan.com*.